Graduate Survival Guide™

Created by Michael Bergman

DISCLAIMER

The Graduate Survival Guide is to be used as a starting point and a general reference tool. This is not a substitute for professional advice. If you have questions or concerns regarding legal, medical, financial, or similar issues you should always contact a professional.

The information included has been obtained from resources that we believe to be reliable. We have done our best to provide an unbiased and truthful guide. We do not make any warranty, either express or implied, that the information is fitting or sufficient for every particular person or situation. The information presented may become out of date. Naturally, the contents are not intended to be used to violate any law. The reader assumes any risk; ultimately you are responsible for your own actions. With the exception of Student Lending Works, whose generosity made this book possible, description of various products, services, websites, and brands are not intended to be endorsements, but merely as references for informational purposes. The authors and the publisher will not be liable for any damages or losses resulting from the contents of this guide or its use.

ISBN 0-9785079-0-8

Graduate Survival Guide™

www.StudentLendingWorks.org

What's Inside

Graduate Survival Guide™ Introduction

You've just graduated and are launching into a completely new life. You're likely to find that your life is changing in many respects-from having a lot of time and little money to having more money and very little time, and from having all your friends living within shouting distance to living in a new place where you may not know a single person. These new experiences and the resulting questions are why this book exists.

Student Lending Works™, a nonprofit student lender, is introducing the Graduate Survival Guide to help college graduates manage the transition from school life to real life. The Graduate Survival Guide was created as a collaborative effort. Professionals (doctors, attorneys, bankers, financial advisors, and engineers), professors and regular graduates helped with ideas, tips and suggestions for making your new life as simple as possible.

With this guide, we look forward to helping you kick start your future. If you have questions or suggestions, desire more resources, or just have some free time on the Internet, check us out on the web.

www.gradsurvival.com

A New
BEGINNING

Why they call it "Commencement"

going to grad school

paying back the man while saving a little for yourself

tips for managing your student loan debt

job search stuff

how to network

what to wear for a formal interview

starting a biz wardrobe and how to match your threads

section
01

3

Going To Grad School

Decide to stall your entrance into the "real world" for a couple more years? Want to get a little more education? Well, before you hit the books again, make sure you consider the following.

Decide On Your Degree

Why do you want to go to graduate school? Do you want a Masters or Doctorate? You'll want to think about how long you'll be in school and what the desired degree will allow you to do afterward (higher paying job, new career opportunity, etc.). Here are some things to think about with some of the popular graduate degrees:

- **J.D. (Law)**
  Where do you want to practice when you're done? You will have a much easier time finding a job in the city where your school is located. Also, think about what bar you want to take, as your school may teach for its state bar. What do you want to do with your degree afterwards, and will this degree help? Is it necessary? Are you ready to work hard for three years? Do you like reading?

- **M.D. (Medicine)**
  No way can you do this without commitment. Are you ready to live at the hospital and function on minimal amounts of sleep? Does the thought of dealing with ill patients or working with cadavers make you violently ill?

- **M.B.A. (Business)**
  What will this degree help you accomplish? Will schools admit you now? Do you have a couple years of work experience?

Test

Once you decide on the degree you want, you'll likely have to take an entrance exam. Some of the main exams are L.S.A.T. (Law), M.C.A.T. (Medicine), G.M.A.T. (Business), and G.R.E. (General Graduate Programs). Check on testing dates, test prep, and the life of your score for your particular exam, as you may be able to use the score for a couple of years.

Money

Grad school will likely mean another couple of years of not getting paid, but the extra degree may open up doors, and will give you negotiating leverage. Also, you will have expenses for living and tuition during your years at school, so make sure you check out financial aid and consider how you will handle the monetary end of graduate school.

Homework
Remember that you will be doing homework or other school activities when your working friends are out having a good time. Then again, you may be on vacation when they are working 9 to 5.

Boards
Depending on your graduate degree, you may have to take boards once, if not several times. Also, you may have to continue taking classes and seminars throughout your life.

Do You Hate Writing?
If your program calls for it, you may have to write and defend a thesis in front of a board. Don't be afraid, but do be realistic.

Before You Do It
Take this step seriously. Sort out the pros and cons and discuss them with your friends and relatives. Your relationships with each will likely be affected by your workload and schedule.

HELPFUL WEB SITES
- www.kaplan.com
- www.princetonreview.com
- www.gradsource.com
- www.studentlendingworks.com
- www.gradschools.com

Paying Back The Man
While Saving A Little For Yourself

So, you've graduated, and all of a sudden your student loan bills arrive in the mail. Guess what... the lenders want their money back. Welcome to the world of Student Loan Repayment. Below, you'll learn what to do with those loans, and how to save some money along the way.

What Loans Do I Have?

Whether you have federal loans or private loans, you'll have to make some decisions about managing what you owe. First, you need to understand the differences between federal and private loans.

Federal Loans

Federal loans, such as Perkins and Stafford loans, can be subsidized (i.e., the government pays interest on your behalf until your loan goes into repayment) or unsubsidized. They allow you up to six months after you leave school before you have to begin making payments. If you return to school before those six months expire, the clock starts all over again. If you go back to school after the six months expire, you can defer your payment, but only during your exact enrollment dates. When you leave school this time, payments are due the next month, not six months later.

Private Loans

Private loans are generally credit based, which means you may need a co-signer, and they have higher interest rates. These rates are typically variable, which means the lender can change the rate at any time. Payment terms are also generally stricter than with federal loans.

To tell if your loans are federal or private, you can look up any federal loans on the National Student Loan Data System website (www.nslds.ed.gov). Through the process of elimination, you can figure out the private loans from the federal loans.

Repayment Options

With federal loans, you may have up to six months to decide how you'll manage your debt. If you have private loans, you may be making your first payment before the ink on your diploma dries. Regardless, here are some good repayment tips:

- If you have a total balance of $7,500 or less in school loans, pay it off, as the longest repayment term you are going to get, 10 years, is all you can expect for a balance of $7,500 or less.

- If you have loans totaling $10,000 or more, consolidate. Consolidating will:
  - Lower your monthly payments; *and*
  - Fix your interest Rate.

What Is Loan Consolidation?

Consolidation is the process by which a lender pays off your individual loans and refinances the total balance into a new consolidation loan with a fixed interest rate and one monthly payment. Because the total balance is often higher, you will have a longer repayment term and your monthly payments will be lower. In addition, if you consolidate during your six-month grace period (if this applies to your loans) prior to entering repayment, your interest rate will be fixed at the lower grace period rate.

Repayment Schedules

When you begin making loan payments, you have a couple of choices to choose from:

- **Standard Payments-**You make the same payment each month until the loan is paid off.

- **Graduated Payments-**For the first two years of repayment, you pay on the interest only, so your payments are low. For the remaining months, your monthly payment increases up to two times more than your monthly payment during the first two years. This is a good idea when you know your salary is going to be increasing significantly over the next two years, but you need to keep the payment low until you get your feet on the ground.

- **Income Sensitive Payments-**Your monthly payment is based on a percentage (%) of your income. (You have to submit income verification each year.) This should be your absolute last resort. The only good thing about this repayment schedule is that your account will not be reported to a credit bureau.

Watch Out For The "Gotchas"

Many lenders make promises, claims and offers to entice you into consolidating with them. In fact, you've probably already been bombarded by junk mail and phone calls regarding various consolidation programs. Keep in mind that they are trying to sell you something. They don't always have your best interests at heart, and they also may not have the best options available for you. Read the fine print. Ask a lot of questions. SHOP AROUND.

Some gotchas and false promises include:

- **No Fees**
  There are no fees associated with federal consolidation loans, regardless of the lender.

- **Permanent Benefits**
  Make sure you see the word "permanent." Know what you have to do to get the benefit and what you have to do to keep the benefit. Typically, lenders will tell you that you get an interest rate reduction after 24 months of on-time payments, "provided that all payments after that are received by their due dates." If a benefit is permanent, it should remain intact, regardless of late payments, etc.

- **Save .06% on your interest rate if you consolidate while in your grace period.**
  There are certain benefits you are entitled to because your loan is backed by the federal government. The six-month grace period is one of these "entitlements." Everyone with a Stafford student loan is entitled to a six-month grace period after graduating or leaving school. During the grace period, the federal government establishes a lower interest rate, 4.7%, which changes to 5.3% when your loan goes into repayment. The difference between these two rates is the "savings" some lenders are offering you. In actuality, this is no savings at all, but rather a grace period interest rate to which you are entitled.

- **ACH (Automatic Clearing House) Or Automatic Withdrawal vs. Automatic Bill Pay.**
  There is a difference. With Automatic Bill Pay, you control when you make your payment; you control what happens to your bank account. With ACH / Automatic Withdrawal, you basically give the lender the right to take money out of your account each month; you do not control when your payment is pulled from your account. And even if you ask your bank to cancel your ACH, it can take up to 10 business days for such a change to take effect.

- **Loan Deferral**
  This is another "entitlement." You are entitled to a temporary suspension of loan payments based on certain events, such as going back to college (called an "in-school deferment") or going into the military (military deferment), just to name a few. Remember, interest continues to accrue during the deferment period on any unsubsidized loans you might have. You don't necessarily have to pay that interest until the deferment expires, but you need to know interest will not stop unless your loans are subsidized.

- **Combining federal loans with private loans. DON'T DO IT!**
  If you consolidate your federal education loans with your private education loans, you will lose all of the federal benefits (entitlements we talked about above). If you want to consolidate, consolidate them separately-federal loans in one place and private loans in another place.

Who Can I Trust?

It's difficult to know exactly whom you can trust. Ultimately, you have to research your lender options. A good place to start is with nonprofit Student Lending Works (www.StudentLendingWorks.org). They can provide you with facts, timely information and loan choices. If they don't have the best option for you, they'll refer you to someone who will. Their website is chock-full of information that will build on the knowledge you've gained from this book. The best part is Student Lending Works isn't working for a huge bank or corporation that's making a whopping profit off of your debt. Instead, they re-invest their surpluses into state education programs that focus on increasing student access to better and higher education, not into stockholder dividends.

HELPFUL WEBSITES

- http://www.studentlendingworks.org
- http://www.studentaid.ed.gov/
- http://www.nslds.ed.gov/ (to get a list of your federal student loans)
- http://www.usnews.com/usnews/edu/dollars/dshome.htm
- http://www.financialaidsupersite.com/about-us.htm
- http://www.usnews.com/usnews/edu/dollars/dshome.htm

Tips For Managing
Your Student Loan Debt

Be Proactive; Find Out What You Owe And Who You Owe

Find out what your total debt is, what kind of loans you have, where they are held, and who you pay. Check this website: www.nslds.com to get a list of your student loans and the details of each loan. Keep records and important paperwork in a safe place.

Make Your Payments On Time

- Paying on time will help establish good credit.

- Paying on time will decrease the total interest that accrues on your loan.

- Delinquencies and defaults on student loans will lower your credit rating, and defaulted loans are turned over to the federal government for collection.

Make Your Payments Affordable

- **Shop for the best benefits.** Many lenders offer borrower benefit programs that can lower your interest rate or reduce your loan principal. Choose the best program for your situation.

- **Choose a repayment plan that works for you.**

  Standard - Monthly payments are fixed with a payment term of up to 30 years. This plan yields the lowest overall interest cost compared to other repayment plans.

  Graduated - Monthly payments are initially lower for the first 2 to 3 years, and then gradually increase over the repayment term.

  Income Sensitive - The monthly payment amount is adjusted annually based on your income.

- **Is consolidation for you?** Consolidation is the process by which a lender pays off your individual loans and refinances the total balance into a new consolidation loan with a fixed interest rate and one monthly payment. Because the total balance is higher, you will have a longer repayment term and your monthly payments will be lower. In addition, if you consolidate during your 6 month grace period prior to entering repayment, your interest rate will be fixed at the lower grace period rate.

  Consolidation Guidelines:
  - You must have more than $10,000 in federal student loans.
  - The loans you wish to consolidate must all be under your social security number.

- Do not consolidate federal student loans with private student loans. If you consolidate your federal loans into a private consolidation loan, you will lose your federal benefits (e.g., fixed interest rate, deferments, subsidized interest, etc.)
- Have your monthly payments automatically deducted from your bank account. Most lenders offer a .25% interest rate discount for choosing the automatic payment method.

Make Your Payments Convenient

- Consolidate your loans (if this is the best option for you) so that you have one monthly payment.
- If you do not consolidate, have your lender combine your loan payments onto one monthly bill.
- Have your monthly payments automatically deducted from your bank account.

Be Informed/Make Wise Decisions

- Some lenders allow you to make monthly payments that are lower than the actual interest that accrues on your loan each month. This will increase your debt to such a level that you may never be able to pay off the principle. Do not choose this option.
- Some lenders offer you "benefits" that are not unique benefits; they are really just entitlements that all student loan borrowers receive from the federal government. Make sure the benefits being hyped are real benefits.
- Don't fall for the "no fees" benefit that some consolidation lenders offer. Actually, there are no fees associated with federal consolidation loans, regardless of the lender.
- When shopping for the best benefits from lenders, be sure that the benefits are "permanent." Some benefits will cease if you have one late payment.
- Another entitlement on your federal student loans is the right to have a deferment or forbearance on your loan if you meet the federal requirements. Choosing a certain lender will not affect this entitlement. Don't fall for lender statements to the contrary.

Job Search Stuff

Have you always wanted to get a job? Have you found yourself with the urge to work long hours and get rid of all that free time? If this sounds like you, or if you've realized you need some money to live, then we've got some great tips to help you get a stellar position.

Employer's Needs
Remember, it's not about you, it's about the employer. What is the employer's timeline? What does their perfect candidate look like? While the employer may be looking at your intellect, personality, and other qualities, you are there to fit their needs at this particular time.

Be Organized
Know your desired job market and track your research, contacts, networking referrals, letters and responses in a notebook.

Get Out Of Your Apartment
Meet people, talk to people, tell everyone you know what you want. Take advantage of resources available on the Internet, but it's those human interactions that will generate the most opportunities. Remember, it isn't just people in high places who have worthwhile contacts. . . the folks you see each day, such as your manicurist or newspaper salesperson, likely have many contacts.

"Boomers"
"Baby Boomers" are the generation that may be hiring you, so put yourself in their mindset. If you are applying for jobs in more conservative environments, think "no visible tattoos" and "no more earrings than ears." Also, lose the "like" from your vocabulary.

Informational Interviews
Seek informational interviews to help in your search. An informational interview is more like a journalist's interview than a job interview, and you are the one asking the questions. Why ask for an informational interview? Because you want to know about your subject's career path, or their occupation, or their employer, or their industry. It's a great way to try on different types of jobs, learn about the skills required, and learn the best ways to break into an industry. All it takes is a healthy dose of curiosity, and professional demeanor and attire. Don't expect a job interview, but you should always be prepared!

Volunteer To Get Experience
Employers don't care if you got paid to get the right experience. Volunteer to get experiences with fundraising, event planning, managing people, writing or marketing.

You can volunteer in your community or with your alma mater. Also, helping others never hurt anyone.

Join Professional Organizations
It is important to join professional organizations in the field you want. This will help you network, fill educational gaps, get great volunteer experience, and enhance your resume. Search online for organizations and local chapters, calendars of events, and contacts.

Seek Advice
Look to friends and family for job advice, as most of them have been there.

The 3 Commandments Of Resume Writing
Perfect spelling, perfect punctuation, and meaningful examples that highlight your experience.

Negotiations
Don't ask about insurance and vacation time until you have a job offer in hand. Remember, it's not all about you at this point.

Some Final Job Search Tips
- It's O.K. to be late when meeting friends for a drink, but never be late for an interview.
- Like your mother always said, "Sit up straight!"
- Work on a firm handshake. While it might sound goofy, a handshake is an important impression, so leave the fish in your 'fridge and begin practicing strong handshakes.
- Don't forget eye contact. Unless you're a recluse writer or computer programmer who never sees the light of day, make sure you make good eye contact.
- Remember that an interview isn't therapy, and it isn't a gabfest with your best friend, so keep some things, like that rash, to yourself.

HELPFUL WEB SITES
- www.job-hunt.org
- www.monster.com
- www.careerbuilder.com
- www.employmentguide.com
- www.gradschools.com
- www.craigslist.com

How To Network

Make new friends. Get a job. Be one of those people who knows EVERYONE. It's all about the networking, baby. Check out some ways to magically turn every person you meet (a bad date, an annoying co-worker, the person next to you on the bus) into a sweet connection.

Use Those Random Connections

For Yourself. If you are interested in working in television and someone says, "My brother-in law's sister works in television..." don't immediately shrug it off. Get the person's name and some contact information. Don't be afraid to send them what may seem like a "random email." Often times, people don't know where to look when they are hiring, and your random email may come at the perfect time. Also, the person you emailed may forward your name to someone else.

For Others. Spread the love if someone sends you a random email. The beauty about networking is what goes around comes around. If people were good to you in the networking process (i.e., gave you names of people, forwarded your resume, allowed you to use their name as a reference) do the same for someone else. It's the right thing to do and it will make the person SO happy.

Go On Lots Of Informational Interviews

* **Initially**
  Call someone who has a job you would like, or that you would like to know more about and ask if you can come in for an "informational interview." Sound interested and be enthusiastic.

* **Preparing**
  Arrive on time, dress appropriately for the position you are applying for (suit if necessary, business casual otherwise, even if the office is super casual) and be awake. Give them something to remember you by. If you have an art portfolio and the prospective job is creative, SHOW them the portfolio.

* **Yourself**
  Make sure you get a chance to talk about yourself and your interests, so they remember you in the future. If you have something really interesting, like you were once a national jump rope champion, mention that—it will stick in their minds.

* **Before Leaving**
  Ask if there are any opportunities available in their company/industry, or if they know anyone who is hiring.

* **Thanks**
  Remember to thank anyone that interviewed you or gave you leads. A handwritten note is always a good way to go. It may cost a little time and money, but it is the

right thing to do and will leave a good impression.

- **Leads**
  Contact the people your interviewer suggested with an email or letter that starts: "I got your name from SO-and-SO. She said you would be a good person to contact with regard to my interest in koala feeding...," and then continue with cover letter- type information.

Just Talk To People

Be friendly with people you meet. They may have somewhat similar professional interests as you. Talk to them, learn their interests - even if you are not going to be best friends with the person, try to keep the conversation and relationship going if they seem like a good person to know professionally. They may be able to connect you with people.

Social outings. Never underestimate the power of a social outing. If you're going out for drinks with coworkers feel free to invite someone you just met who works in a related industry. People in the real world are less hung up on social conventions and usually won't think it is weird if you invite them out based on one meeting. Everybody loves a good networker - everybody wins; you may make a new friend, and even if you don't, you've made an impression on them (hopefully a good one.) You are no longer a resume and a name. You have a face. It is beautiful. And it is going places.

HELPFUL WEB SITES

- www.careerkey.com
- www.careerkey.com/networking_resources.htm
- www.careerjournal.com/jobhunting/networking
- http://my.monster.com/NetworkingSearch/Search.aspx?searchtype=keyword
- www.quintcareers.com/networking.html

What To Wear For A Formal Interview

When you went to get that job at Señor Burger's or Captain Coffee's, you probably didn't have to worry about shining your shoes or matching clothes. Well, you've grown up and so should your interviewing attire, unless you're going back to the kitchen.

Formal Atmosphere

If you're looking for a job in a formal atmosphere (law office, accounting firm, consulting company, etc.) you probably should wear a suit. A good rule is to dress just like you would for work, so, make sure you're dressed the same as or a little better than the employees. If the employer has a human resources department, see if they can help you out.

Men:

- **Suit** – You should wear a dark suit (navy, charcoal gray, or black). These colors are clean and professional looking. The suit should be classic style with two or three buttons. If the suit is more than 3 three years old, consider going shopping, as styles change every couple of years.

- **Shirt** – For interviews wear a white shirt that is professionally laundered. You don't want to call attention to yourself because you look like you slept in that shirt, or because that purple shirt is so odd. Always wear a long sleeve shirt; there is no such thing as a short sleeve dress shirt. Spread collars, as opposed to button collars, are more professional.

- **Ties** – Colors that are classic and rich looking, such as maroon or gold are safe bets and complement your dark suit and white shirt.

- **Shoes And Socks** – With a dark suit you should wear black lace-up shoes with black or navy socks.

- **Belt** – Your shoes and belt should match, so go with a black belt if you're wearing black shoes.

- **Accessories** – You shouldn't wear too many pieces of jewelry, perhaps a watch and a ring. You really don't want to call attention to yourself. You don't want the interviewer to remember you as the guy with earrings and necklaces everywhere. Don't wear jewelry that jangles.

- **Cologne** – Wear a minimal amount. You don't want people from 4 offices over commenting on your scent.

- **Misc.** – Consider bringing a leather portfolio, which may include your resume, blank paper, pen and any questions for your interviewer.

Women:

- **Suit** – The best way to dress for in interview is to wear a conservative suit - nothing too flashy or edgy. While some of you might want to show more of your personality through your style, an interview is often not the best place to do so. You do not want to distract the interviewer from your skills and your purpose for being there. Therefore, wearing a black, navy, or charcoal suit would be the safest route to take.

- **Blouse** – You can't go wrong by having a nice, crisp, clean white blouse which would match any suit color. If you do want to spice up the look a little, consider a blue hued blouse. With black or charcoal suit, you can take your look even further with a pink blouse

- **Shoes** – Instead of flaunting your strappy stilettos, an interview is a time to break out the dusty closed-toed shoes. You are best off wearing a black, well-polished pump. You do not want the heel to be too high where you might trip or hurt yourself or others.

- **Pantyhose** – Your safest choice of pantyhose colors would be a nude tone or black sheer. It can't hurt to throw an extra pair in your briefcase or conservative looking purse.

- **Makeup** – You want a clean, fresh look. You do not want to show up looking as if you're a member of the circus. Your eye makeup should be subtle; do not overdo the eyeliner or blue eye shadow. Lipstick should be apparent but not too flashy - no bright bright reds.

- **Hair** – You want to keep your hair pulled back, away from your face. You do not want to have stray pieces in your face, as this could tempt you to play with your hair and distract the interviewer.

- **Accessories** – Elegant yet simple. Body or facial piercings are not recommended for standard interviews. Carry your resume in a leather portfolio. It is best to come prepared with paper and a pen. Therefore, your best bet would be to purchase a portfolio that includes a notebook. You might want to bring any questions you came across in your research of the company you're interviewing with you in this portfolio as well.

- **Perfume** – Although you might have the best perfume money can buy, others might not share the same opinion. Therefore, no perfume is the best.

HELPFUL WEB SITES

- www.menswearhouse.com
- http://interview.monster.com/featuredreports/polish/
- www.quintcareers.com/dress_for_success.html
- www.job-interview.net/interviewlibdress.htm
- www.worktree.com/tb/IN_dress.cfm

Starting A Biz Wardrobe & How To Match Your Threads

On the way to a big time job and want to get started off on the right foot? Don't know where to begin? Check out the list below to aid in your shopping needs and tips to remember.

What Should I Buy To Create A Basic Business Wardrobe?

For Men:

- 3 White shirts with point collar
- 2 Blue shirts with point collar
- 1 Black belt
- 1 Pair black lace-up shoes
- 3 Pairs of solid black socks
- 3 Pairs of solid navy socks
- 3 Suits
  - 2 button or 3 button classics styles
  - Colors such as navy, charcoal, black
- 2 Ties per suit
- 7 Days of undergarments (underwear and crew neck shirts)
- 1 Blazer (either black or navy)
- 2 Pairs of slacks (1 tan and 1 gray)
- 1 Black raincoat (long)

Just a little extra help for those guys who still have trouble matching.

	Navy Suit	Black Suit	Grey Suit	Brown Suit
Shirt	white blue	white blue tan	white blue	ecru white blue
Tie	gold maroon purple	grey/silver maroon gold	maroon/black grey	shades of brown navy multi-brown
Socks	black navy	black grey	black grey	brown
Belt	black cordovan	black	black cordovan	black cordovan
Shoes	black cordovan	black	black cordovan	black cordovan

For Women:

- 3 White blouses

- 2 Professional colorful blouses - ex. light blue, bright blue, pale pink

- 3 Tasteful/neutral shells you can wear under a suit jacket if you're not in the mood for a blouse. This piece can also be worn alone with a pant or skirt. Recommended colors: black, white, blue, beige.

- 1 Pair black leather pumps - make sure the heel is not too high

- 5 Pairs of nude panty hose - in case of "runs" it can't hurt to leave an extra pair at work

- 3 Suits - depending on the dress code you're best off purchasing jacket and skirt suits, but if there is an option to purchase the suit with all three pieces (jacket, skirt, and pant) go for it. With these three basics you can constantly mix and match.
  - You can never go wrong owning a black suit. It can take you anywhere.
  - Colors such as navy, and charcoal are also wonderful staples

- 7 Days of undergarments (underwear and proper bras)

- 2 Pairs of slacks (1 black and 1 grey)

- 1 Black raincoat

- 1 Black and 1 brown tailored belt

FOR ALL: Things To Remember

- Get your shirts professionally laundered.

- Take care of your shoes (replace heels, replace laces, polish them, etc.).

- Dry clean clothes as little as possible, as its both good for the fabric and your wallet.

- Always hang clothes up properly, giving them time to rest (never at the bottom of a closet).

- Buy the best you can afford and always look for sales. You are better off purchasing a well-made basic product (i.e. suits, rain coat) that will last you years than a poorly made one that will fall apart in months

- Your work wardrobe is a valuable investment that helps you on a daily basis

- Don't be afraid to ask questions at the store. Salespeople will be able to help you match, get good deals, and watch out for your wardrobe wants/needs.

- Don't over accessorize.

- For men, match your belt buckle with your watch.

HELPFUL WEB SITES

- www.josbank.com
- www.nordstrom.com
- www.macys.com
- www.brooksbrothers.com

MOVING YOUR STUFF, AND A ROOF ABOVE YOUR HEAD

section
02

How To Pack Your Stuff

Now comes your favorite part of every move, packing. Who doesn't love spending hours wrapping an entire ballerina and clown figurine collection in bubble wrap and separate boxes, only to unwrap them two days later? Here are some quick hints to get you packed up prim and proper.

Plan

Where are you moving? Will you be taking your stuff around the block or across the country? Think about how far your stuff will have to travel and plan your packing accordingly. The farther the trek, the more chances your stuff can break. Also, consider if you'll be moving to a place with a lot of stairs or on the ground floor. Plan your box weight and size according to the practical realities of the move. Finally, don't save your packing until the last minute.

You vs. Moving Company

Who will be carrying all this stuff? If it's you and your friends, you'll want to think about everyone's weight limit. You may want to consider stacking things by weight and marking boxes according to weight, as well as contents. Moving companies may charge extra for extremely heavy objects, so check beforehand.

Boxes

You'll definitely need some boxes for your move. Nobody wants to pay for boxes, so plan. Think about what sizes you need. Start gathering them a couple of weeks before you're ready to pack. Big stores with shipping docks should be able to help you. Ask for permission to take boxes and make friends at the dock, as maybe they'll spot boxes for you. Grocery stores stock at night, so check them out late. Also, tell your friends that you're on the lookout for boxes and ask them if they'll put them aside for you.

Specialty Boxes

While you may be able to corral enough free boxes for your move, remember that certain items may need special packaging, such as artwork and awkward sized items. Check out office supply stores, shipping companies, and moving companies for specialty boxes.

Wrapping Material

While you could buy bubble wrap at an office supply store, you may want to save a couple of bucks and use newspapers, or even old English composition drafts that have mysteriously piled up in your drawers. Save old school newspapers, or the "what's happening in _____" that are free at every restaurant. Toilet paper and paper towels are good for glass, as are bathroom/kitchen towels. If you use towels you'll be accomplishing two goals at once, packing them and protecting other goods.

Tape

Make sure that you have enough packing tape. You don't want to be running out every 10 minutes to buy more. Since you'll inevitably need to use it in the future, grab the big roll.

Markers

You'll want to mark your boxes with contents, weight, destination, etc. Get a couple of those big permanent markers that smell up your whole place.

Scissors

It's very likely that you have a pair lying around, but if you have friends helping you, maybe ask them to bring a pair too, or pick up a cheap pair, so that you don't spend your day passing sharp instruments back and forth.

Snap A Photo

If you're adept with digital cameras, you may want to snap a picture of each box's contents. You can keep the pictures for your own files (in case anything breaks) and also stick a copy on the box, so you can easily determine the boxes contents.

HELPFUL WEB SITES

- http://interiordec.about.com/od/moving/a/org_movetips.htm
- www.mayflower.com/moving/full-service-movers/moving-tips/packing-tips.htm
- www.vanlines.com/packing_guide
- www.homestore.com/Move/Planning/Packing/Default.asp?poe=homestore

Moving Tips

Now comes moving day(s), which are usually really long and really tiring. You get to look forward to fun-filled hours of carrying stuff, loading things, unpacking, driving, and sweating. To ease your life and maybe save some money, here's some info that will help out in your move.

Hiring A Moving Company

Make sure you do your research if you are going to have the pros move you. Don't settle on the first company you call. You should call at least 3 companies to get quotes and information. You should also ask friends that have moved recently who they used and if they were happy. Look for national companies for moves over a long distance. Here are issues you need to bring up:

- **Charges:** Do they charge hourly, on a flat rate, or in another manner? Don't be afraid to negotiate. They have the truck and the employees, and if they don't have a move that day, then some income is better than no income. Also, see if they give free estimates.

- **People:** Ask them how many people will they need to move your stuff (tell them what size place you are moving out of and where you're moving to).

- **Dates:** Find out if they're available on your moving day, and, if you're moving far away, when your stuff will get there.

- **Insurance:** Ask the company if they are insured or bonded.

- **Packing:** If you are in a time crunch, ask if they'll pack for you and how much it would cost.

- **Vehicles:** If you need to ship your car, find out if they can handle such a move, the cost, and delivery date.

- **Tab:** See if your employer will pick up the tab or if they have a relationship with a moving company.

Renting A Truck

Plan ahead if you're going to move yourself. You'll need to plan a couple of weeks ahead to rent a truck. Check for availability, as weekends are usually busy. Ask the rental company if they have weekday v. weekend specials, and if they offer any specials for AAA or certain credit cards.

Other Equipment

Remember to get blankets for fragile items and a dolly for large pieces.

Friends

If friends aren't there to help you move, then they're not really your friends. If you were smart and made friends with people who drive trucks and SUV's, ask them if they wouldn't mind moving a box or two. To make sure they remain your friends afterward, pay their gas and feed them.

Storage Lockers

You should think about getting a storage unit if your new place is smaller than your present digs, or if you're not sure where you're going to move permanently. Some things to consider include:

- **Location:** Where do you want to store your stuff?

- **Price:** If possible compare prices of several storage companies. See if they have specials for certain times of the year, or for membership in certain organizations.

- **Availability:** Plan ahead. Start making phone calls and visits to storage companies at least several weeks ahead of your move to make sure they can accommodate you.

- **Length Of Time:** How long will you need the place? See if you can go month-to-month, or if you are locked into a long minimum term.

- **Size Of Unit:** Before you ask them what size unit you need, ask them for availability and what types of pieces you can fit in each unit. Measure your stuff and check out each unit. Mentally and/or physically plan how you will pack the unit.

- **Access:** Find out when you can access your storage unit. Will it be 24 hours a day, or will it be limited hours?

- **Insurance:** Call your insurance company before you move stuff into your unit and see if they offer coverage. Your storage company may also offer insurance, so compare prices and consider what you'll be storing, and its value.

- **Heated/Air Conditioned:** If you have items that need to be in a temperature-controlled unit, expect to pay more than for an un-regulated unit.

- **Security:** Find out what type of security they have.

Movable Storage Units

If you don't want to have to drive your stuff to a storage unit, you can have your unit driven to you. It's possible to have storage units delivered to your place. You fill it up, have it taken back to the storage facility, and delivered when and where you need it.

HELPFUL WEB SITES

- www.realtytimes.com/rtnews/rtcpages/20000927_movingco.htm
- www.bbb.org/alerts/article.asp?ID=229
- www.uhaul.com
- www.ryder.com
- www.publicstorage.com/servlet/MainServlet?page=/index.jsp
- www.putitinapod.com

Moving Checklist

Moving is a big change in your life and you want to make it as easy as possible. To help you with the transition, here are important things to think about in the weeks leading up to moving day.

Packed Up
Sounds simple, but how many times have you found that extra "surprise" in the corner of the closet? So, make sure you go through you place with time to spare.

Moving Day Is Planned Out
Decide whether you want to do a lot of little trips yourself along with a big moving day or if you just want to hire a moving company.

- If you decide to use a moving company, understand the contract, confirm the details and make sure they know where your place is and what time to arrive.
- If you're going to hire a truck, make sure you plan accordingly.
- If friends are going to help you, make sure that you thank them with food, drinks, and plenty of sugar.

Your New Place Is Ready
You want to make the transition as smooth as possible, so confirm that you can get into the new place right away, that your lease is signed, and you can get the keys.

Utilities Are A Go
You won't want to spend your first night without electricity, heat, telephone, high speed internet, or cable (how cruel could they be). Contact all the proper companies so that all is up and running when you move in.

Renters Insurance
If you choose to protect your stuff, make sure that your renters insurance is set for the day you move in.

Deliveries
If new furniture or appliances are being delivered, you will want to confirm the delivery dates a couple of days beforehand. You should think about what order you want everything to go into your new place; you'll want to have a dresser to put your clothes into or an entertainment cabinet for the TV.

Cleaning Supplies

You'll want to make your new place feel like it's yours. A good advance cleaning will make the place seem as new as possible. Stock up with paper towels, rags, and cleaning fluids. If you are moving cleaning supplies with you from your old place, know where they are and make them easily accessible.

Donations

Moving is a great time to assess what's been piling up in your drawers and closets. If you still have your M.C. Hammer pants, maybe you should think about donating them to those who grew up deprived of such an exciting wardrobe. If you keep track of their value and donate them to a qualified charity, you may receive a tax deduction.

Pets

Don't forget man's best friend. Consider the kitty's comfort, or the dog's dilemmas in changing scenery.

Closing Up Shop

Make sure you forward your mail, disconnect old utilities, close bank accounts, and inform the landlord in a timely manner that you'll be moving (time period will depend on your lease and the city you live in).

Remember

If moving to a new city/state, remember to update your voting information and to find out the details on getting a new driver's license and plates.

HELPFUL WEB SITES:

- https://moversguide.usps.com/?referral=USPS
- www.2c.com/wb_hrpages/hr_gen_moving.html
- www.century21.com/learn/content.aspx?refstr=6.8.7

Picking Where You Want To Live

The time has come to pack up your belongings, hug your friends goodbye, and say adieu to your college stomping ground. But where are you going? Here are some things to consider before moving on.

Ready To Leave?
If you had a good college experience it may be hard to leave. If you're considering staying in town, think about your reasons. Life will be different as people leave town and your work schedule differs from your school schedule. Evaluate your chances to check out other cities and weigh your lifestyle opportunities in various places.

Life Is A Journey
No doubt that you will receive countless offers: 1) move back in with ma and pa (yikes!), 2) move with a college friend to a new city, 3) join a cult (please avoid), 4) live with a friend or relative in a new city who will put you up for a bit, or 5) keep the status quo. You'll be O.K. whatever you choose, so don't let fear make your decision. Check out a new city, try a new career path, or live in a new apartment.

Job? Don't Be Afraid To Get Out Of Town
Let's say you've received a job offer. It sounds awesome, but you'd have to move to a city/town where you don't know anyone. Really, what have you got to lose? If you hate it, move again. At least you can say you tried.

Be Realistic
Does the area you select have opportunities in the field you've chosen? If you haven't chosen a field, does the area have enough to offer so that you can explore your options?

Give It Time
Change can be hard, and challenging. You may feel lonely, lost, confused, and melancholy for the good-old days, but in time you will make new friends, find new places to go, and become comfortable.

Become A Nomad
Now is probably the best time in your life to explore the U.S. and the world. You have your education behind you, your life ahead of you, and minimal responsibilities.

Help Others
If you're not sure where you want to end up, consider helping those who are less fortunate than you. Check out teaching/volunteer opportunities in the U.S. and abroad.

Evaluation 101
Picking a place to live mimics in many ways the drills you went through in choosing a college. You will need to consider if you want to be a big fish in a small pond or a small fish in a big pond. Also, think about what type of social life you're looking for, job prospects, and traffic.

HELPFUL WEB SITES

- www.usps.com/moversguide
- www.liveabroad.com
- www.teachforamerica.org
- www.msmoney.com/mm/career/job_hunting/first_job/picking_location.htm
- www.findyourspot.com
- www.money.cnn.com/best/bplive

How To Find An Apartment

So you just moved to a new city or finally moved out of the dorm? Finding a place to live might seem a little overwhelming at first, but it is generally easy to do. There are many options to consider when searching for the right apartment, but follow the tips below and you will be in the perfect place in no time.

Starting Points

If you are unfamiliar with the city, do not know anyone already living there, and have no idea where to start, then check out apartment finding services that are free of charge (they usually get their fees from the apartment). Also, look online for information about apartments. Some cities have apartment brokers and roommate referral services. Also, many grocery stores have free apartment guides.

Where Should I Live?

Location is one of the most important factors when you select an apartment. Consider proximity to highway or public transportation and proximity to your office or graduate school. How close are friends, the bars, restaurants, the gym and other social areas? Where is the nearest grocery store?

Roommates

If you are going to live with someone else you should consider work schedules, eating habits (will you be sharing food?), party life, and what you each want in a roommate (a check, a best friend, or an acquaintance).

How Much Should I Pay For Rent?

A general rule of thumb is that you should be able to afford between 19-25% of your gross annual income. Shop around at a few apartment complexes or buildings to get a feel for the range of rents in your area. The cost of an apartment will vary within different parts of the city. Generally, the more amenities the apartment offers (like a gym, pool, security systems or gates, laundry facility, etc.), and the newer the facility, the higher the rent will be.

Negotiations

Rent is not set in stone, so negotiate. Use rates from other similar places in the area and find out if any specials or deals will be coming up soon. Lease terms can also be negotiated.

Application Fees

Some apartments will charge a one-time payment when you submit an application. Be sure to ask the leasing agent about this; sometimes apartments will waive the fee.

Referral Fees

If your apartment complex is offering referral fees, find a new neighbor and split the cash.

Security Deposits

Almost all apartments will charge a security deposit that must be paid when you sign the lease. The deposit is held by the landlord until your lease ends and will be used if there is any major damage to the apartment. If there is no major damage, besides ordinary wear and tear, your security deposit should be given back to you shortly after your lease ends. Check your state laws if a problem occurs with the return of the deposit.

Notice To End Your Lease

Ask the leasing agent and read the lease carefully to determine how much notice you need to give when either terminating the lease or communicating your intent not to renew the lease. The apartment will almost always require written notice. Make sure you give written notice (calling the leasing agent will not suffice) and make sure it is within the proper time period; otherwise, your lease may automatically renew and you could be stuck with hefty financial penalties for breaking it.

Can Fido Live With Me?

Make sure you know whether the apartment allows pets and whether there is a certain weight limit (for dogs). Many complexes will allow common pets (fish, birds, cats, or dogs) but will likely require a deposit in advance. This deposit often is in addition to the deposit the apartment ordinarily charges and is typically returned if there is no damage.

Washing Clothes

If you do not own a washer or dryer, ask to see if the apartment has a laundry facility or even provides a washer and dryer in your apartment. If not, there are services which rent washers and/or dryers, or you might consider buying one. Also, make sure the apartment has the necessary washer and dryer hookups.

Utilities

Most apartments will provide you with information and phone numbers for the utility companies. You will need to call them (phone, power, gas, cable, etc.) and arrange a time for them to come to your apartment. Also, remember to check out exposure for satellite dishes and the availability of high-speed internet access.

HELPFUL WEB SITES

- www.apartments.com
- www.apartmentguide.com
- www.craigslist.org/about/cities.html
- www.rentnet.com

Renters Insurance

Although often overlooked or ignored by many people, renters insurance is both very cheap and very valuable. It will help protect you against damage to your belongings from fire or smoke, lightning, vandalism, theft, or water damage from plumbing. Just as important, renters insurance will protect you from any damage your neighbors might have caused - if their apartment floods above you, your stuff could be damaged as well. The price of renters insurance is usually well worth the money!

Where Do I Buy It?
If you already have auto insurance, talk to your agent. Most insurance companies sell renters insurance.

Live In A House?
Renters insurance usually will cover any losses in an apartment or rented house.

Cost
The average cost for renters insurance is only $12 a month for about $30,000 worth of property coverage. Obviously, prices will vary from city to city and depending on the coverage amount. You can increase the coverage amount for relatively small sums. Your coverage will be for the total cost of all of your possessions, not on an item-by-item basis.

Payment
Usually you can pay monthly, but some insurance companies will charge you every six months or yearly, which may be cheaper in the long run.

Roommates
Check with your local insurance provider to see how to handle roommates and your insurance policy.

"Actual Cash Value" Or "Replacement Value"
In a loss, actual cash value will pay you whatever that particular item was worth. Replacement value will repay you the cost for replacing the damaged/ lost item with a new, comparable item. So, for example, if a couch you paid $500 for three years ago was damaged, the actual cash value might be only $150, while the replacement cost would be closer to what you paid for the item.

Deductible

A deductible is the amount you pay out of your own pocket in the event that your possessions are damaged. Once you pay your deductible, the renters insurance policy kicks in. So, if you have a $500 deductible, and there is $3,000 worth of damage, you will pay for the first $500 in damages and the insurance company pays the remaining $2,500 (assuming the total amount of damage is within your policy). Generally, the higher the deductible, the lower the cost of your monthly premium payments. However, you need to first assess whether you can afford to pay a higher deductible in the event something is damaged.

What If My Landlord Has A Policy?

The landlord's policy will cover only the structure of the house or the apartment, not your belongings. Only your policy will cover your belongings.

Determining The Price Of A Renters Insurance Policy

Some of the factors include the area in which you are living (if it is prone to thefts), the structure of your building, whether you have a security alarm, smoke detector, or fire extinguisher, and if your area is gated.

Do I Really Need It?

Add up the cost of your furniture, electronic equipment, CD's, jewelry and personal property; can you afford to replace all of that if it is stolen or damaged? Shop around for the best renters insurance policy. It is cheap, but worth every penny!

Moving

Remember to cancel/transfer your policy when you move. You might even get a refund.

HELPFUL WEB SITES

- www.apartments.about.com/od/rentersinsurance
- http://personalinsure.about.com/cs/renters
- www.insurancefinder.com/homeinsurance/rentersinsurance.html

Hiring A Real Estate Agent

Do you love salespeople? Do you want to drive around with them in your free time and have late night chats with them? Think about medical assistance. If, though, you are itching to put down roots and buy a house or condo, you'll probably look for a real estate agent for help. Here are a few guidelines to assist you.

Who's Your Boss?
Confirm who's representing whom. Remember that many agents are acting on behalf of the seller. Their initial duty is to the person listing the property. If you want a buyer's agent make sure that person is indeed your agent.

The Search
Call real estate companies in the area. Seek referrals from friends, relatives, or business associates, and ask them about their personal experiences.

Reputation
Make sure the representative works for a company with a good reputation. This person is representing you in dealing with others, so consider their reputation yours.

Check Out a Few
Interview several prospective representatives. Ask about the market. Are they up-to date on pricing and trends?

Getting Along
Try to find an agent you personally like. See if he/she shares your philosophy, needs and wants. Is this person trustworthy? Remember the agent will help you make one of the biggest investments of your life, so feel that you can trust them and work with them in negotiations.

References
Don't hesitate to ask for references, and make sure you check them out. You'll want to know how the agent performed and how helpful they were.

Priorities
Before entering into a relationship make sure that you all are on the same page in regards to house types, pricing, timing, and community attributes.

Commission And Obligations

Remember that generally the seller pays the commission. Make sure you have no legal obligation to the agent who you choose. Get it in writing. Before you sign anything make sure to consult with an attorney.

Other Ways An Agent Can Help

Use your agent as a source for lenders, housing inspectors, contractors, and other services you'll likely need when buying a place.

Availability And Dedication

Find out if the agent is a professional or just someone who is dabbling on the sidelines.

> " Not a flock of wild geese cackles over our town, but it to some extent unsettles the value of real estate here, and, if I were a broker, I should probably take that disturbance into account. "
>
> Henry David Thoreau

HELPFUL WEB SITES

- www.servicemagic.com/article.show.moving-and-storage.checklisthiring-a-real-estate-agent.10163.html
- http://public.findlaw.com/real_estate/nolo/ency/0CE75422-F17C-45E0-A938D973A0B7AAFB.html
- http://bbb.org/alerts/article.asp?ID=225
- http://bbb.org/alerts/article.asp?ID=209

Purchasing A Condo Or Townhouse

You've graduated college, got a job, and now want a "Real Place." Condos aren't solely for your grandparents and can be a nice investment. Here are a few pointers to help you find a suitable condominium/townhouse.

Condo/Townhome
A townhome is often a multi-story residence that shares a common wall, while a condominium can be defined as an apartment building in which each apartment is individually wholly owned and the common areas are jointly owned.

Location
Do some research about the town where you will be moving. By doing this you can familiarize yourself with the area and figure out ideally where you would like to live (close to work, school, family, etc.) Location is a especially important when purchasing a condo or townhouse.

Size
Make sure the place will be of adequate size for you and/or roommate(s). Prices of condominiums will vary according to size.

Budget
Depending on your budget, look for places that are relatively new and well built or that have been maintained well. Get a professional inspector to advise you. This will pay off in the long run, since maintenance fees and repairs may pile up later.

Condominium Fees
Most condominium complexes have a home owners association (HOA) fee that may be paid on a monthly basis. This usually covers any exterior maintenance, pest control, pool maintenance, etc. Be sure to check how much these fees are and work them into your budget.

Utilities
Some condos and townhomes include some utility fees in the HOA (i.e. water, cable, etc.) Make sure you check to see which ones, if any, are included. Also, you'll want to see if you can have a satellite dish, or access to a communal satellite dish.

Appliances
Make sure appliances are in good working order, especially if they are older. If new, check whether they meet your specifications.

Finance

Make sure to check your financial status before proceeding. Talk to local mortgage brokers and/or banks to see what you can afford. Many brokers will perform a preapproval before you find a place, so you'll know what you can afford when it's time to start shopping. There often is an application fee with this service.

Condominium Layout

Look for condominium units on the upper floor(s) - this is especially useful if you pick an older complex, as less chance for flooding and is safer from a break-in standpoint. Units on the lower levels will experience quite a bit of noise that can be very annoying over time. On the other hand, if you want to have more leverage in negotiations, consider using the placement of the condo as a bargaining point.

Comparison Shop

Try to compare a variety of complexes in a logical way. If you are adept with computers, try to put together a spreadsheet analysis of the various places.

Demographics

Figure out if your potential new place is consistent with your lifestyle needs. Do you want a fitness center, pool, young singles as neighbors, a place to raise kids, etc.?

Parking

Parking is very important for both you and guests, so see if you have a dedicated spot.

Exit Strategy

It's not too early to think about leaving yourself open to new options or opportunities. Think about what would happen if you wanted to move. Are there a lot of condos built around the same time as yours? Are you buying in an up-and-coming area? Will your place be appealing to others?

HELPFUL WEB SITES

- www.hribar.com/how_is_buying.htm
- http://loan.yahoo.com/m/primer14.html
- www.allspect.com/condo.html
- www.realtor.com

YOU'RE MOVED IN
NOW GET OUT

how to find good restaurants

how to find a good bar

joining groups

spas

picking movies

concert tips

getting politically active

golf stuff

how to pick an athletic club

how to pick a tennis club

fan life–tips on sporting events

education throughout your life

section
03

How To Find Good Restaurants

So you lived on peanut butter and jelly sandwiches, pizza, and insane quantities of caffeine for 4 years. Now that you're really out on your own, buffets will not be available for every meal, and you'll probably want to try some meals that don't feature the word "fried." Here are some tips for picking restaurants.

Decide What You Want

In order to have a good dining experience, you should figure out what you're looking for. Think about the following attributes when deciding on a place:

- **Size Of Your Party**
  Do you want a special room, special seating, will there be a long wait because of your party's size?

- **Food Quality**
  Is food quality the most important, or can you settle on a place that has just O.K. food, but a great atmosphere?

- **Dining Experience**
  Are you looking for a fine dining experience or a place where you can be loud with your friends?

- **Bar Atmosphere**
  Do you want a restaurant that has a bar?

- **Reservations**
  Think about how much time you have for your meal and whether reservations are necessary.

- **Menu**
  What range of foods do you want? Are your mates vegetarians? Do they have dietary restrictions?

- **Wine List**
  If you are looking to dine well, what kind of wine list does the restaurant have and is a sommelier available to help you choose a bottle?

Ask Friends

Your friends often have similar tastes in food or at least have an idea of what you like and don't like. Tell them what you're looking for in a restaurant and see if they can help you out. Try to get a couple of names so that you can choose based on location, reservation times, or type of food.

Ownership

If you dine at a restaurant that you enjoy, see if the owners/operators run other restaurants in your area. You can find out by asking, looking at the bottom of the menu for logos, or by taking a peek at the business cards often found at the hostess stand.

Newspaper

Most city papers have restaurant reviewers write up at least one restaurant a week. Keep your eyes open for these, or even check out the archives on the internet. Besides the major newspaper, check out the arts/entertainment newspapers in your city (they're usually free), as they may review trendier or smaller restaurants.

Local Magazines

Many large cities have local magazines that run articles, reviews, and pictures about things happening around town. Most of these periodicals run at least one food issue per year.

Internet

The web is a great resource for finding restaurants. You can check out online reviews, locations, menus, and comments about restaurants without leaving your seat.

City Guides

In many cities, restaurant guides are organized by type of food, expense, and attire, along with food descriptions. Check out your local bookstore for them.

Other Sources

If you like road side joints or fancy dining, you can likely find a book that will give you restaurant names not only in your city, but also throughout the country.

Concierge

If you're at a hotel with a concierge, take advantage. They have a vast knowledge of the restaurants of the city, so tell them what you're looking for and let them help you.

Email

If visiting a new city, email your friends prior to your departure and ask them for suggestions. It's more than likely they have been there or know someone who has.

HELPFUL WEB SITES

- www.citysearch.com
- www.mobiltravelguide.com/index.jsp/index.jsp/index.jsp;jessionid=5E9B8C36 E33EE830050B5B2EA4A7C?menu=rating&bodytid=102
- www.restaurantrow.com
- www.fodors.com/reviews/drevselect.cfm

How To Find A Good Bar

In college, finding a bar was pretty easy. You went where everyone had been going for years. Everyone had their regular hangout, where they went week after week to feel comfortable and relaxed. Now, out of college and in the working world, you probably will need to find new places to grab a pint and play some darts.

What Types Of Places Do You Like?
To find what you consider a good bar, you should think about what you want.

- Quiet atmosphere to talk with friends, or a loud, hopping bar?
- Do you want to dance all night long or just chill in a pub?
- Do you want beers and drinks from all over the world, or just the old same bottle of the popular brand you can get anywhere?
- Do you want to dress up or go in jeans?
- Do you want to be surrounded by people your age or a crowd of various demographics and ages?
- Do you want to play pool, darts, or watch sports?
- Do you want live music or just a jukebox?

Ask Around
Asking around is a great place to start. Find out where your co-workers and their friends hang out. Ask your waiter in restaurants or a person at your health club. It's always fun to find new places that you'd never heard of.

Try Them Out Yourself
Take a couple of friends and go on a night of barhopping, trying place after place to see what fits. Places with the long lines outside are usually a good place to start.

Check the Phonebook
If you're looking for something special, like beers from around the world, check the yellow pages for bars that advertise such specialties.

Concierge

If staying at a hotel, ask the concierge or front desk attendant to recommend a place. Even if you're not staying at a hotel, drop by one and ask the concierge for their suggestions.

Girls/Guys

If you're interested in finding that special guy or gal, then forget everything above and just look for attractive people.

66 *It's better to sit in the bar and think of church than to sit in church and think of the bar.* 99

Swedish proverb,
translated by Verne Moberg

HELPFUL WEB SITES

- www.barcrawler.com/search.htm
- www.citysearch.com

Joining Groups

Now that you're on your own and out of school, you may need to work a little bit on meeting new people. You'll likely feel most comfortable with people who share your same interests and ideals.

Think About What You Like
Are you a knitter, an athlete, involved in politics, a musician, a poet, or involved in religious organizations? If you have a hobby or interest and want to pursue it after college, or want to take up something new, think about how involved you want to be, how much time you have, and how far you are willing to travel.

Check Out Their Stomping Ground
If you want to be involved in improv, local theatre, music, religious groups, tennis leagues, etc., think about where such groups gather. Check local papers, school newspapers, bulletin boards at coffee houses, churches, synagogues, etc.

Ask Around
If you are new to a town and want to become involved, seek out people at work, at your apartment complex, or at the coffee shop. You can discover their take on certain groups or even find out about other things to do.

Internet
Use the internet to find resources. Check out the city's web site along with national websites that may list local groups.

Old Contacts
If you were involved in activities at school or in your old city, ask the organizers if such groups exist in your new area.

Co-Workers
Ask co-workers if your office is affiliated or belongs to certain organizations. You may even broach the idea of organizing some groups (bowling leagues, softball leagues, pub crawls, etc.) through the email system or the bulletin board at work.

Yellow Pages
Use old school resources, like the yellow pages, to find places of interest to hang out or organizations.

College Campuses

Hit the local college campus to see what organizations they have open to the community. Look at bulletin boards and postings throughout the campus. You may also want to take a look at a college phone book and give interesting organizations a call to see if they are open to the community.

Check Service Opportunities

Community service activities are great places to meet others. So volunteer in your community and meet some great people and help out others at the same time.

HELPFUL WEB SITES

- www.sportandsocialclubs.com
- www.citysearch.com
- www.worldkickball.com
- www.volunteermatch.org
- www.meetup.com
- http://groups.myspace.com/index.cfm?fuseaction=groups.categories

Spas

Spas are not just for old, rich ladies and "health nuts," but for everyone. So, relieve some of the stress of trying to watch two TV shows at once and go somewhere to relax.

Clear The Decks
Make sure your calendar is free of commitments. You want to have a guiltless and enjoyable time, so find a couple of hours when you don't have meetings to rush off to.

Get The Facts
Choosing a spa will often depend on your budget and the amenities and services you want. Referrals are often a great way to find a spa, so ask friends and co-workers. If you want a woman or man to do your massage, make sure you confirm this prior to going.

Do A Pre-Check
If you are spending a lot of money at the spa, ask about the amenities they have (blow dryers, shower facilities, beverages, meals, magazines, etc.).

Check With Your Physician
If you suffer from medical conditions, check with your doctor to get a clearance.

Preparations
Drink plenty of water to avoid becoming dehydrated from the treatments. Find out in advance if there are other preparations should be made prior to going for your treatments.

Know Your Treatments
Here are some of the more common treatments:

- **Aromatherapy Massage**
  A massage using scented oils.

- **Bodywrap**
  A treatment where your body is wrapped in strips of cloth that may be treated with herbs.

- **Facial**
  A treatment for the face that may include toning, moisturizing, and exfoliation.

- **Shiatsu**
  Japanese massage technique to provide relaxation.

- **Swedish Massage**
  Plant and flower extracts are used to massage away pain and provide relaxation.

> " *If a man insisted always on being serious and never allowed himself a bit of fun and relaxation, he would go mad or become unstable without knowing it.* "
>
> Herodotus

HELPFUL WEB SITES

- spas.about.com/library/blsitemap.htm
- spas.about.com/cs/spasitecontents
- www.spafinder.com
- www.spaindex.com

Picking Movies

Have your friends banned you from choosing movies, or was the last movie you saw so bad that you couldn't stop looking at your watch? Do you always get the worst seat in the house and never get a discount? If you want to stop wasting time and money then keep on reading.

How To Pick A Winner

A great way to find movies that you will like is to do your research. Check out magazine reviews and newspaper reviews of movies. If you find a movie critic who you've agreed with in the past, see what they say about a movie before checking it out. Try to find a synopsis of the movie so you get a feel for what the movie is about. You may want to avoid movies during the opening weekend, so you can find out other's reactions to the movie before you plop down $10 on a bummer.

Key Parts

Many movie advertisements mention the writers, directors, screenwriters and actors, so - take note of this information. If you liked a movie by the screenwriter, then you probably will enjoy his/her other stories. If you enjoyed the fast paced action of the director, then you might enjoy his or her next offering. This is a good way of weighing the odds in your favor.

Buying Tix

It seems that movie prices have gone up faster than the values of a Picasso. If you're savvy, though, you can still save some money.

- **Matinees/Early Bird Specials**
  Many theater chains offer cheaper prices for movies that you see before 6 p.m., so if you want to make it an evening of dinner and a movie, think about checking out the movie first and dinner later.

- **Student Discounts**
  Some chains offer student prices on all movies; make sure to ask (assuming you're eligible) if these discounts exist.

- **Frequent Viewers**
  If you go to a certain theater chain a lot, ask if they have any membership programs, where you can earn free movies and concessions.

- **Coupons**
  Various organizations offer coupons that can save you a couple of bucks per show. While you may have to pay for a booklet of these coupons, they are usually well worth it if you go to movies often. Some such organizations are AAA and The Entertainment Book.

- **Automated Box Offices**
  Many theaters have installed these machines, which can cut down on lines and let you get to your movie faster.

Hate Craning Your Neck?

If you hate getting the last seat in the house and having to sit three miles away from your friends, then get to know your theater better. If it's opening weekend on the big $100 million show, then likely it will be a full house, so get there early. If your theater is in the middle of a huge shopping center, consider parking issues you may face. Finally, if you hate crowds and like watching movies in intimate settings, think about going to movies at off hours and off days, such as 10 p.m. on Monday.

Problems At The Theater

If you have any problems at the movie theater, i.e. bad framing, out of focus picture, bad sounds, etc. complain to the manager- they'll likely give you comp tickets without hesitation.

Check Out Your Local Campus

Many colleges and universities have movie nights/special screenings, where they may have discount movies, foreign films, or festivals.

Watching At Home

As technology gets more advanced, home movie seeing becomes easier and easier. Ask your cable/satellite provider about movies on demand, where you can order movies from a library over your cable/satellite system. Also, if you hate running out to the video store, check out mail order programs, where they'll send DVD's to your door.

HELPFUL WEB SITES

- www.entertainment.com/discount/movie_tickets.shtml
- www.aaa.com
- www.netflix.com
- www.movies.com
- www.imdb.com

Concert Tips

If the last live concert you went to involved puppets and everybody singing happy songs, while you and your third grade class drank juice and ate cookies, then maybe you should get out a little more often. Live music is the best way to experience a band, so grab your juice box and check out some concerts.

Finding Shows

- **Internet**
  Sites, such as Pollstar.com allow you to search cities, venues, or artists to help find a show worth seeing. You may also want to look at sites that focus in on what's going on in your city.

- **College Campuses**
  Live music is a integral part of the college campus life, so if you're near a campus, check out their newspapers, bulletin boards, or web sites to see what's going on nearby.

- **Band Web Sites**
  Log on to band web sites to find out if they'll be nearby. Some sites even allow you to join email groups, where you'll be notified if they're coming in your area.

- **Newspapers**
  Check out local newspapers, whether they be the mainstream news type of paper or an alternative publication.

Spending Your Money Wisely

A great way to experience music at a great price is to go to music festivals, where you can buy a day/multi-day/week pass to see many different types of bands. During the spring and summer, many cities such as Memphis, Atlanta and New Orleans have such festivals. A great festival/conference where many new artists are discovered is Austin's South by Southwest. Finally, many colleges bring artists to campus to play for their students for free or very cheaply, so you may be able to see a great headliner for a couple of bucks.

Buying Tickets

The internet makes ticket purchasing much easier than having to stand in line, but the old fashioned method still works in some cases, such as when shows are in such demand that internet purchasing slows down. In such times, think about out of the way ticket sales spots, such as out of the way grocery stores, where no ticket-desiring concertgoer would ever look (beware, though, that since they get less ticket traffic, workers may not be as familiar with the sales process). If you want to save a couple of bucks, you may be able to avoid handling charges by purchasing the tickets at the venue. You may also be able to get early access to premium seats by joining a band's fan club, and such clubs may even lead to meet and greets.

If Sold Out

Seats for shows that sell out in the first couple hours will often show up at the ticket seller a few days later as credit cards get rejected. Also, promoters will sometimes open up new blocks of seats to sold out shows a few days before or the day of.

What To Bring

If you're going to an outdoor show, think about bringing bug spray, blankets, trash bags (if the ground might be wet), and sunscreen. Check with venues before hand if you want to take photos, as each will likely have their own policies. Finally, if you want to buy drinks, food, or concert goodies remember to bring a lot of cash.

HELPFUL WEB SITES

- www.pollstar.com
- www.sxsw.com
- www.myspace.com
- www.blender.com/tours
- www.ticketmaster.com
- www.usatoday.com/life/columnist/popcandy/2004-05-25-popcandy_x.htm

Getting Politically Active

Now that you've spent the overwhelming majority of your life learning about everything, why not go out and put it to use — vote. Here are some tips on registering to use one of the greatest powers you have.

Note: Voting varies throughout the country, so make sure you find out the details where you live.

Where Can I Register To Vote?

A registration application can be obtained from the local election officials in your county. You can also register online, through outreach programs sponsored by various organizations (e.g. The League of Women Voters), when applying for services at state DMV or driver's licensing offices, and at state offices providing public assistance. Also, many states offer registration opportunities at public libraries, post offices, unemployment offices, public high schools and universities.

When Can I Vote?

Poll opening times usually range from 6:00 a.m. to 8:00 a.m., while closing times are usually between 6:00 p.m. and 9:00 p.m. Again, all of this varies by state, and sometimes by county and town within the state.

Where Is My Polling Place?

Polling place locations in each community are determined by local election officials. For the location of your specific polling place, contact your county election official who may be either the County/Municipal Clerk, Supervisor of Elections, or Board/Commission of Elections.

Requirements

Most states require that, in order to be eligible to vote in an election, you register 20 to 30 days beforehand. Other specific state registration requirements vary, but below is a sample of some of the requirements your state may have:

- Must be a U.S. citizen.

- Must be a resident of the state you wish to vote in (and sometimes the county or municipality where you plan to vote) at the time of registration or a number of days preceding the next election.

- Must be 18 years old or turn 18 prior to the election.

- Certain past criminal convictions (e.g. felony, bribery or treason) may bar you from voting.

- Some states require that you swear or affirm various things such as to uphold the Constitution or that you are a qualified voter.
- Must not be registered to vote or claim a right to vote in another state or jurisdiction.
- Must not currently be declared incapacitated or incompetent by a court of law.
- Must not have been convicted of corrupt practices in respect to elections.

QUICK facts

Term Of President	4 years (2 full terms max)
Presidential Elections	Every four years
Number Of Senators	100
Term Of Senators	6 year terms with staggered elections
Number Of Representatives	435
Term Of Representatives	2 years

HELPFUL WEB SITES

- www.fec.gov
- www.rockthevote.com
- www.declareyourself.com
- www.vote-smart.org
- www.senate.gov
- www.rnc.org
- www.drudgereport.com
- www.instapundit.com
- www.wonkette.com
- www.democrats.org
- www.whitehouse.gov

Golf Stuff

Despite knickers or other goofy outfits, golf is still a great sport. You can play golf with your friends, your girlfriend or boyfriend, parents, or business associates. In order to make sure you're par for the course, check out the following list.

Finding A Course
Decide how serious and committed you are to playing golf regularly. If you don't want to worry about the hassle and odd tee times at public courses, consider joining a golf club. Check out their membership rates and initiation fees. If you only want to play a couple of times a season, then public courses are your best bet. Ask your friends and co-workers where they play, then compare notes.

Equipment
If you don't have your own set of clubs, now is a great chance to get a set. After all, you're now making money and probably will be using them in the years to come. You should demo a couple sets before purchase. Everyone has different likes, and everyone's game is different. It's a good idea for a golf pro to fit your game with a certain type of clubs. If you decide that new clubs are too pricey, hit the internet and second-hand sports equipment stores for a bargain. You could also talk a sibling, friend, or neighbor into getting a new set and donating their old set to a good cause — you.

Learning The Game
Golf is a game of rules, so become familiar with the rules of the game. Your reputation in playing golf can follow you into the business world, so play with friends who know the game or pick up a copy of the rules. There are also good videos that help teach the fine points of golf.

Getting A Sweet Swing
Taking lessons can get expensive, but is a great way to get a smooth swing that will be with you forever. If the budget is tight, see if your pro will do group lessons or find out if any organization, such as a college in your area, offers the community golf lessons. Hitting the range often will help you feel more comfortable with your game. If you plan on going to the same range a lot, ask if they have any membership deals or frequent customer programs.

Pricing
Golfing is not a cheap sport, but if you shop around on tee times you can save money. Find out if the course has weekday specials, twilights specials, or cheaper times on weekend afternoons. Also, make sure to see what is included in the price (ie. cart, caddy, pull cart, etc.)

Tee Times

When deciding on courses to play you should look into their tee time availability and how they determine priority. Find out when they open tee times for the weekend, and if you can make tee times over the internet, or if you need to call.

Handicap

If you plan to play with any frequency you should get a handicap. This evens out the playing field between average players and scratch (very good) golfers. Ask any golf course where you play how to start gathering scores to get a handicap.

Golf Trip

A great way to get together with a group of friends and share a relaxing activity is to organize a golf trip.

Golf Schools

If you really want to get better quickly and are willing to spend a little of your hard earned money, think about going to a golf school. There are many schools throughout the U.S., especially in Florida and in the Western U.S., where you can get great instruction and have a fun trip.

HELPFUL WEB SITES

- www.usga.org/rules/index.html
- www.usga.org/associations/index.html
- www.who-golf.com
- www.espngolfschools.com

How To Pick An Athletic Club

Where can you get a workout, listen to music, and find attractive people? The gym, you fool. Here you'll find some things you should look into when finding a place to drop down your money and some sweat.

Location
Is the club close to home and/or work?

Hours Of Operation
Are the facilities open 24 hours? Are there peak hours when all the machines are full?

Parking (if applicable)
Will you have to spend half your allotted workout time looking for a parking spot?

Amenities
Does the club have food, locker rooms, a spa, dry cleaning, juice bar, etc?

Cleanliness
What are the locker rooms like? Are the machines well kept? Is it well lit?

Number Of Members
What is the club like at its fullest capacity? Do you have to wait for machines?

Personal Trainers
Does the club offer personal trainers? What are their qualifications? How long have the trainers worked there?

Orientation
Is there an orientation for the club, so that you become more familiar with the machines, facilities, programs, etc?

Events
Does the club offer special events for singles, families, or have recreational leagues?

Fees
See if your employer/school has an affiliation with any club in particular. Look at clubs later in the month as they may try to fill up quotas and be more flexible in negotiations. Try to negotiate on any initiation fees.

Membership Agreements
Make sure you read the contract fully, taking notice of the length and terms of the agreement.

Guest Fees
What will it cost if you want to bring in a non-member? Are there incentives if you recruit new members?

Cancellation Policy
Find out what types of notices, charges, penalties etc. are applicable if you want to get out, need to move, or found a better deal across the street.

Background
Check out the background of the club, so that you don't get ripped off if they go under. Also, find out if they have reciprocal agreements with other clubs in town or elsewhere.

HELPFUL WEB SITES
- www.healthclubs.com/choosing/body6.html
- www.healthclubdirectory.com
- www.ihrsa.org
- www.24hourfitness.com
- www.lafitness.com

How To Pick A Tennis Club

Unlike football, tennis is a great lifetime sport that people of all ages can enjoy. Think about it. Do you see people your parents age playing football with friends? No, they play tennis, and have been doing so for years. Now that you've got a little more free time, spend some of it getting better at this great social game. Follow these tips when looking for a club to improve your skills.

Location
How far is the club from home and work?

Type Of Club
Is the club strictly a tennis club, or is it an all-purpose facility that offers golf, racquetball, fitness, etc.

Membership
What types of packages do they have? Are there monthly dues? Is there an initiation fee?

Court Fees
Explore pricing during peak and non-peak times.

Guest Fees
Do they exist, and if they do how much? How many times are guests permitted to play?

Courts
How many courts does the facility have? What type of courts do they have, i.e. clay, grass, hard, indoor, outdoor, etc.

Availability
How do the styles of membership affect court availability? Does one type of member have priority over another?

Cleanliness And Amenities
How clean are facilities and how are the courts kept? Do they offer a racquet shop that can restring your racquet? Do they have a locker room? Do they have ball machines?

Programming
What kinds of programs are offered? Do they have group lessons, private lessons, in-house leagues, traveling teams, and tournaments?

Opponents

How easy is it to find people to play? Is it easy to find people to play singles and doubles? Does a posting board/email list exist so that you can find playing partners?

Lessons

Consider the following tips before taking lessons.

- Number of professionals employed by the club.
- Are various lesson times and types (private or group) available?
- Is the instructor USPTA or USPTR certified?
- How long has the instructor been employed at that particular club?
- How long has the staff been in the tennis industry as a whole?
- Ask the desk staff who would be a good on-court instructor.
- If you know a member of the club, ask for a recommendation.

HELPFUL WEB SITES

- www.uspta.org
- www.ptrtennis.org
- www.usta.com

Fan Life - Tips On Sporting Events

Question: What's better than sitting on your couch and watching the game? Hint: It's not mowing your lawn. Answer: Attending one. Nothing beats the sights and sounds of a live sports event. Also, where else can you get a $5.00 hot dog to complement your $10.00 soft drink? If you are going to be a spectator - do it right.

Tickets

Scoring tickets depends on supply and demand, along with your desire for certain seats. If you want to be guaranteed good seats for several games, look into season tickets or special packages your team offers. If the game is sold out or you want to live on the edge, go down at least a half-hour before the game and see if anyone is scalping tickets. Prices should go down the closer to game time. If scalping tickets, check with your local laws to find out where and at what price scalping is legal. Another way to get tickets is through a broker or internet auction.

Attire

Check the weather before going down to a game. If it's cold, a safe bet is to layer, and bring a raincoat if there's a chance of showers. If you don't want to lug a raincoat around, think about bringing garbage bags to make makeshift ponchos. Remember, many stadiums won't allow umbrellas. Finally, if you're a die-hard fan, throw on your jersey and face paint.

What To Bring

Some items to consider: seat cushions, binoculars, your own food/drinks (if venue allows), camera, sunscreen or handwarmers, bug spray, and a cell phone so you can call your friends and brag how great your seats are.

Learning A New Game

If you're going to your first professional basketball game or first polo match, you may want to do a little homework on the rules.

Tailgating

Have a bunch of friends and want to make the game an event, then pack up the car, head down early and tailgate. Make sure your food is relatively easy to prepare (or prepared beforehand), that you remember garbage bags, that you have wipes/hand sanitizer, and that you bring enough food for your new friends who will wander by the party.

Getting On The Tube

If part of the pleasure is getting your face on TV, consider face paint and costumes. Also, patriotism plays well, so dress up as Uncle Sam or bring a flag.

Some Great Events:

- Superbowl
- World Series
- The Masters
- The U.S. Open
- The Final Four

- Wimbledon
- The Stanley Cup
- College Bowl Games
- The Olympics
- X-Games

HELPFUL WEB SITES

- www.packer.com/tailgate
- www.rulescentral.com
- www.expn.com
- www.superbowl.com
- www.ncaasports.com

Education Throughout Your Life

Are you planning to let all your hard-earned brain cells go to waste and become mush, like that carton of Chinese food in the back of your fridge that you blame on your roommate? To avoid becoming a walking two-week-old sweet and sour chicken, you should think of education as an ongoing, lifelong process. No, it doesn't have to be particle physics or finance for Wall Streeters, it can be a fun skill such as woodworking or photography.

Local Colleges
Check out local colleges in your area to see if they offer night or weekend courses. Classes may include contemporary topics, computer skills, or various types of sports or music lessons.

Online
With the increasing use of the internet and growing technology, schools and companies are offering online courses and degrees. You could learn new computer applications for home and personal use, or you could get certified in a specific field, allowing you to further your career.

Community
There are many people out of school who strive to expand their horizons and those of others. Check out some of the following places for classes, lessons, or workshops in your area:

- **Bulletin Boards**
  Look at your local library, city hall, coffee shops, grocery stores, bakery, or anywhere else that has postings. You could even put up a flyer advertising your interests in a particular field (ie. learning to knit or starting a book club).

- **Newspapers**
  Besides your city's daily newspaper, look in community papers to see if there are any classes that interest you.

- **Cities/Townships**
  Sometimes governments offer educational programs. Places that could have information on such activities include: local schools, city halls, county or township administration buildings, or town newsletters.

- **Workshops/Co-ops**
  See if local art workshops or co-ops in your area offer courses.

Yellow Pages
Have an interest in welding, glass blowing, or dog grooming? Check out your local yellow pages for classes or businesses that might give you information on training or seminars.

Recorded Courses
Who says you have to leave your home to become educated? You can now get courses taught by famous teachers on CD, audio tape, and DVD. Never had the chance to take philosophy or world history? Now you can while sitting on your comfy couch.

Computer Programs
Check out the software section of your local store or the internet to find programs that can teach you history, new languages, or how to program computers.

Podcasts
Schools, professionals, and amateurs are creating lecture series in the form of podcasts that you can download to your MP3 player or computer.

HELPFUL WEB SITES

- www.universityofphoenix.com
- www.teach12.com
- www.languageadvantage.com
- www.podcast.com
- www.itunes.com

MONEY, MONEY, MONEY

section
04

Budgeting

If you've become hooked on infomercials or have ordered everything the Franklin Mint has put out, you may need to do a little reality check, not only to your personality, but also to your spending habits. As you begin earning paychecks and dealing with your own finances, now is a great time to become financially organized and budget minded.

Philosophy Of A Budget

A budget is made up of two parts - cash in and cash out - and an appreciation of where you stand in each area will help you. Before deciding what to include in a budget, decide how strictly you need to adhere to your set allotments. If you tend to spend a little frivolously, you may want to a budget to serve as a warning signal, letting you know when you're getting out of control. If, on the other hand, you are very conservative with your money, use a budget as a loose guideline.

Getting Started

Try to look at your existing patterns of spending and earning to help form the outline of a future budget. Get out your check register and paid bills as resource data, along with old tax returns and worksheets. Start by listing all of your cash in (earnings, gifts, etc.), along with your monthly cash outflow to get a firm grasp on what you should be spending each month. There are many types of computer programs, such as Quicken and Microsoft Money that can aid you in keeping track of your budget. You can even download your account information and sync them with your financial software, giving you up to date info at your fingertips.

Expense Categories

Important categories for expenses will include:

- Housing
- Food
- Utilities
- Household Expenses
- Educational
- Clothing
- Loans
- Insurance
- Gas/Transportation
- Travel
- Entertainment (books, CD's, DVD's, Movies)
- Charitable Contributions
- Health and Medical
- Misc.

Putting It Together

Once you've gotten your list of cash in and cash out, go ahead and add them up. Most likely, you will find that your expenses are devouring the money coming in. Take a pencil and try to trim. Look for categories that beg for a little discipline. Once you've worked out a realistic set of numbers, write them down and start to see if you can live with what you've created.

Savings

Don't plan on spending all of your inflow, because at that rate you'll never get to retire or be able to deal with the bumps that life may bring along, such as unemployment, sickness, or family emergency. When planning your budget, attempt to save as much as reasonably possible for the future; you may even consider setting aside an established percentage each month.

Living Within The Budget

Once you've set up your parameters, try to live within them as much as possible. Keep track of your cash flow either on computer or in a notebook and see how well your projected budget has worked out. Don't be afraid to make changes to your budget, but also recognize that you may need to change too. For example, if you find you're constantly spending more than you anticipated think about cutting the unnecessary expenses, i.e. eat one more meal a week at home instead of dining out or park in a cheaper parking lot, even though you may need to walk a little further.

HELPFUL WEB SITES

- www.finance.yahoo.com
- www.personal-budget-planning-saving-money.com
- www.budgetingonline.com

Financial Planning Tips

Do you remember your parents having long and boring conversations about planning for their financial future? Well, now it's time for you to start having those long, boring conversations, but at least you'll be the one enjoying life on the beach when all those conversations pay off.

Emergency Reserve
As soon as possible, you'll want to build up a 6-month reserve fund in case of layoffs, job transitions, or unexpected events. This should cover bills, rent, and insurance. Make this an account that is not easily accessible, so you won't be tempted to use it for frivolous spending. Consider a money market fund, acquired through a bank or mutual fund company.

Save First
It is wise to take out your savings when you first get each paycheck, instead of spending first and saving whatever is left. Pick a certain amount to save every month and stick to it. Remember, the more years you save money, the more interest it will earn for the future. If you are between the ages of 25-30, you should consider saving at least 10-15% of your gross income.

Budget Wisely
Once you get all moved in to your new place, sit down and form a budget. Stick to it, as it will help you handle your day-to-day living expenses and it will allow you to save for the future.

Diversify
You'll likely want to diversify your assets between stocks, bonds, and cash. Through diversification you can minimize your exposure to financial loss. If you're not a savvy investor, consider using mutual funds as a way to diversify.

Reduce Income Taxes
Figure out how to reduce your income tax, whether by setting up retirement accounts, participating in your retirement plan through work, or contributing in a deductible IRA. There is never a wrong time to consult with a local CPA (certified public accountant). They will generally save you more than they cost.

Be Aware Of Risks

Depending on your investment, risk is involved.

- Prices could decline in the stock market.

- Interest rates could drop, decreasing income from CD's, saving accounts, and bonds.

- Diversification risks if you don't have a balanced portfolio. For instance, if you only have tech stocks in your portfolio, you have a greater risk of having all of your stocks decline at the same time due to impact on the tech market. If, though, you own tech stocks along with auto stock, financial institution stock, and oil company stock, a level of protection is established since some sectors may advance while others fall.

HELPFUL WEB SITES

- www.finance.yahoo.com
- www.personal-budget- planning-saving-money.com
- www.budgetingonline.com

Banking Tips

If the closest you've gotten to a bank in recent memory is a visit to the ATM to get cash for those Stone's tickets, then you've got to know your bank a little better. Below are some key terms and basics you should know to help you get more out of your bank and your money. That, in turn, can get you front row seats, as opposed to those nose bleeds you had.

Banking Terms

- **Interest**
  This is the dollar cost that a borrower pays a bank for the use of the money. Also referred to as the "rate," interest varies from bank to bank and from credit card to credit card. The rates are set by the Federal Reserve Board, sometimes referred to as the "Fed." Banks borrow money from the Federal Reserve and then lend it out to their clients. The rate they are charged is called the "Discount Rate." The difference between the discount rate for the banks, and the rate they charge consumers is called the "spread." This is how banks make money. For example, if the discount rate is 2% and you get a loan for 7%, the bank is making 5% on that loan. Rates to look for in the news are the discount rate and the prime rate. The prime rate is the rate the banks charge their best customers. Being aware of these rates will help you when negotiating with a lender.

- **APR**
  The cost of credit on a yearly basis expressed as a percentage. This may differ from the actual rate because fees are included.

- **CD**
  This is a Certificate of Deposit. A form of time deposit at a bank or savings institution. This type of time deposit cannot be withdrawn before a specified maturity date without being subject to an interest penalty for early withdrawal. Small denomination CDs are often purchased by individuals. Large CDs of $100,000 or more are often in negotiable form, meaning they can be sold or transferred among holders before maturity. The rates are posted at the institution. They are typically available for a few days up to as much as 10 years. The rate you get is guaranteed, and the longer the term, the higher the interest earned on the deposit.

- **Commercial Bank**
  A bank that offers a broad range of deposit accounts, including checking, savings and time deposits, and extends loans to individuals and businesses. Commercial banks can be different from investment banking firms, such as brokerage firms, which are usually involved in arranging for the sale of corporate or municipal securities (i.e. stocks and bonds).

- **Credit**
  The promise to pay in the future in order to buy or borrow in the present. It is also the right to defer payment of debt.

- **Credit Card**
  Any card, plate or coupon book that may be used repeatedly to borrow money or buy goods and services on credit. Examples are MasterCard, Visa and American Express.

- **Credit Score**
  A record of how you borrow and repay debt. It is a statistical system used to determine whether to grant credit by assigning numerical scores to various characteristics related to creditworthiness. Sometimes referred as your "Beacon Score" or "FICO" score. Establishing and maintaining a good credit score is very important. It will determine whether or not an institution will lend you money, and at what rate. Companies such as Equifax, TransUnion and Experian track this information. You can establish credit by getting a credit card and repaying on time. You can establish your own phone bill, utility bill and medical bills to create a credit score as well.

- **Debit Card**
  A card that resembles a credit card but which draws money from a checking account, with the transfers occurring instantly after your purchases. A debit card may be machine readable, allowing for the activation of an automated teller machine or other automated payments equipment.

- **Points**
  In reference to a loan or mortgage, points consist of a lump sum payment made by the borrower at the outset of the loan period. Generally, each point equals one percent of the loan amount.

- **Variable Rate Loan**
  A variable-rate agreement, as distinguished from a fixed-rate agreement, calls for an interest rate that may fluctuate over the life of the loan. The rate is often tied to an index that reflects changes in the market. A fluctuation in the rate causes changes in either the payments or the length of the loan term. Limits are often placed on the degree to which the interest rate or the payments can vary.

Paying For Services

- **Checking**
  Most banks will advertise free checking. This is usually for a specific period of time. Ask what minimum balance you need to maintain to continue to receive the free checking account.

- **Savings:**
  Same as above, most banks will require a minimum balance to ward off any fees.

- **ATM Cards**
  Fees are usually waived if used at the institution's ATM. Otherwise you may be charged a usage fee to use the ATM to withdraw your money. Be careful, if you withdraw $10.00 from a foreign ATM, you may be charged as much as $2.00 from that institution and another $1.50 by your bank; you are paying 33.5% to withdraw the funds.

Reasons For Choosing One Bank Over Another

Today, most banks will offer very similar services. Ask about fees and on-line service capabilities with electronic bill payments. Go to the websites of the various banks and see what services are offered. Placement of branch offices can be important. However, with online services, you may never have to go to a branch other than to open your account.

" Money alone sets all the world in motion. "

Maxim

HELPFUL WEB SITES

- www.ing.com/us/individuals/index.htm
- http://bbb.org/alerts/article.asp?ID=307
- www.transunion.com
- www.equifax.com
- www.bankrate.com/brm/defhome.asp

Obtaining And Keeping Good Credit

While you may think that good credit is only necessary when you want to buy that new dress or that flat screen television, it actually is more serious than that. Check out the tips below to keep your credit strong, so that you can get the clothes, TV's, and houses, you've always wanted.

What Is A Beacon Score?

The Beacon Score is the "score" by which all consumers are measured. This is an accumulation of your past five to seven years as a borrowing consumer. This one measurement can make or break you when you want or need credit for both personal and business reasons.

Credit Cards

These can be both a blessing and a curse. It's good to have a credit card on your credit report. If handled properly, they enhance your beacon score. That means... NO late payments, NO over-limit spending, and NO accounts "closed by issuer." An additional "NO" is NOT too many credit cards. Having too much credit available can be a negative as well. Credit issuers view this as excess capacity that might get you in trouble later.

Tips For Keeping Credit Card Debt Under Control

- Don't use it unless you can pay off the balance at the end of the month.

- Keep an eye on your rate; most start out low but will increase after the introductory period.

- Pay on time, and understand that in some instances paying during the grace period is still considered a late payment.

- Don't fill out multiple credit card applications. They may offer you cool free t-shirts on campus or a great discount on clothes at the department store, but it's not worth the negative impact on your credit. (see Inquiries below)

- Save cards for emergencies. As a recent graduate, you may not have a lot of savings built up, but emergencies still happen that you will have to try to be prepared to deal with. You may have a medical issue, car problems, or a broken computer that you need to fix right away, but don't have the large amount of cash required to pay for it. Still, make sure you can cover that expense later in the month when the payment comes due.

- If you cannot pay off your balance, after exhausting every effort to do so, at least pay in excess of your minimum payment.

Installment Loans

These are for those purchases such as furniture, automobiles, televisions, washer & dryers, and other large item purchases that often signed for at the store. But BEWARE, those "same as cash" deals carry a LOT of interest. It's hidden within the terms & conditions. Plus, both the store and the finance company are "betting" on the fact that you won't pay it off when the "free" period is over. NEVER look at the payment amount. These are sold to you as X number of easy payments. Look instead at the APR. (Annual Percentage Rate.) These tell the real story. It might be cheaper to finance it on a 15% credit card versus a 24% APR easy payment plan. But like credit cards, NEVER be late on these payments and NEVER pay during "grace" periods, as they still count as late payments.

Mortgage Loans

First of all, you won't get to this point if you don't have a decent Beacon Score in the first place. But when you do, how you pay this loan is very important to your credit. The theory is that you'll pay THIS payment before you pay anything else. So late payments on this particular credit are viewed as a problem.

Late Charges

If you are EVER assessed a late charge and it looks like an error, do NOT ignore it and just have the late fee reversed. Insist that the credit issuer reflect the payment as made on time and have them send you something in writing to verify this after the error has been corrected. You have RIGHTS. These are listed under the Fair Credit and Reporting Act. You can ask for and receive a copy of any company's credit policy. It's boring reading, but it might come in handy if you ever come up against a credit issuer with an attitude.

Medical Bills

Late payments on these might be as a result of many different things, from insurance to late billing by the service provider. But they CAN appear as negative credit on your account. If you EVER have to "make payments" on a medical bill versus paying it in full, be SURE you make it clear with the service provider's collection agent that it reflect a payment plan, that the payments are current, and that it does NOT show as delinquent on your report.

Inquiries

It might not seem like a major issue, but when you're out car shopping and you get qualified at four car dealers for credit for that new car purchase, every credit inquiry that is sent in by car dealers after the first one counts against you! This sends a signal through the credit system and every inquiry after the first one LOWERS you Beacon Score. These inquiries are based on a set number of inquiries within a set period of time. It varies with different credit bureaus, but suffice it to say that more than one every couple of months sends up a red flag. The thought is, "Is this person getting into TOO much debt?" So be careful with this as ALL credit grantors watch this carefully.

Everything Counts

A final thought to remember is that everything counts both FOR and AGAINST you in the credit world. There is no "neutral" thing you do. This is all set up with numbers & ratios and is based on history. So when you do anything in the world of spending money ... just keep in mind that "It counts." This includes things such as paying taxes, insurance, dental bills, or the trash man.

Steps To Take If You're Already In Over Your Head

- Just like with student loans, it's possible to consolidate your monthly credit card payments into one monthly bill. There are many consumer credit organizations, as well as banks, that will do this. Again, you have to be careful when choosing who to consolidate with, and understand that getting another loan or working with such an agency can affect your credit negatively.

- Transfer debt from another card onto a card with a lower interest rate. Only do this if it's not going to bring you close to or over your limit.

- Renegotiate with your creditors. Creditors will do what they can to protect themselves against the total loss of you filing for bankruptcy. This may mean lowering the interest rate, or a lower repayment schedule. If you don't feel comfortable doing this yourself, there are organizations that will do it for you.

- Examine what you do have (probably as a recent graduate, not too much) in savings, a 401(k), life insurance, home equity, and family help. It may hurt to use this money so early, but if you can avoid going through the lengthy, complicated and expensive process of bankruptcy, it's worth exhausting every option.

HELPFUL WEB SITES

- www.cccsoc.org/pages/credit_guide/credit_guide_07.phtm
- www.quickenloans.com/mortgage/articles/credit-guide.html
- www.nea.org/money/pf030604.html
- bbb.org/alerts/article.asp?ID=617
- bbb.org/alerts/article.asp?ID=616
- www.bankrate.com
- www.nslds.org
- www.howstuffworks.com
- www.italladdsup.org
- www.creditcardguide.com

Advice For Doing Your Taxes

Does April 15th haunt you deep to the core of your being? Hopefully not, and if it does perhaps you should consider counseling. But if April 15th does make you wince, then you're a normal human. The following will hopefully make tax time a little less painful.

Software

If you have a simple return, tax software can allow you to do your own taxes. If you work in one state, and your main source of income is a W-2, you can prepare your own.

Services

If your tax return is a little more complex, check out inexpensive tax services or even full scale accounting firms, depending on the complexity of your return.

Hiring An Accountant

Be prepared to pay several hundred dollars for a quality accountant. Word of mouth is a good way to find a practitioner, so ask co-workers, family friends, parents, etc. Look for a practitioner who suits your personality, as some are more aggressive than others.

Due Date

April 15th is the due date (postmarked). Returns can be extended twice, once until August 15th and again until October 15th. This does not mean that your payment is extended. The estimate of your tax is due in April.

Self Employment

You are responsible for self-employment taxes on income received as a freelancer (FICA and Medicare), so save your money to pay on April 15th.

State Tax Returns

Most states require you to file a state tax return, so check with your state's tax office. You are required to file multiple returns if your home is in one state, but you work in another. Some states don't have personal income tax, such as Florida, Texas, and Nevada.

Student Loans

If your adjusted gross income is less than $65,000 for a single return or $135,000 for a joint return, you may be able to claim a special deduction allowed for paying interest on a student loan. Consult a tax professional or the IRS to see if you qualify.

Deductions/Exemptions/Credits

Deductions and exemptions reduce your taxable income but does not result in a dollar-for-dollar reduction. Credits, though, actually are dollar-for-dollar reductions.

Exemptions

You get one exemption (for yourself); make sure your parents aren't claiming you.

Deductions

Mortgage interest, state income taxes, charitable contributions up to 50% of your adjusted gross income, real estate taxes, and medical expenses over 7.5% of your adjusted gross income are all deductible.

Filing

Depending on marital status, you can file in the following manners: single, married filing jointly, married filing separately, and head of household.

Retirement Accounts

401(k) and Traditional IRA's are deducted for adjusted gross income (not taxed until you take them out, but a penalty of 10% may be applied). For Roth IRA's, your money is taxed now and tax-free when taken out.

Gambling

Gambling winnings are taxable, but losses are only deductible up to gains.

Capital Gains

Sale of stock is taxed at a lower rate than wages and other income. A "gain" is the sale price (less commissions), less the price you paid for it (including commissions).

Investments

You are required to report interest and dividends from investments, such as stocks and bonds. The proper form for this is a 1099, and it is very likely that your brokerage house will provide it.

HELPFUL WEB SITES

- www.taxcut.com/taxtips/tax_terms/glosstoc.html
- www.bankrate.com/brm/itax/news/20020917a.asp
- www.hrblock.com/taxes/index.html
- bbb.org/alerts/article.asp?ID=341

Mutual Funds

*Want to brag to your friends how you have ownership in all the "Big Companies,"
but lack the necessary funds to make your claims? Then check out mutual funds.
Oh yeah, they're good for other purposes besides being a bragging jerk.*

Definition
Pooling of investments by a number of people. A fund manager manages the funds.
The fund can invest in stocks and bonds, as well as other investments. Imagine
a fund as a grocery bag filled with various goods that represent different types
of investments.

What Do I Own?
A portion of the fund.

Determination
When researching mutual funds, look into the fund manager and that manager's
history.

Family Of Funds
There may be an advantage to buying within a family of funds, as they may allow
transfers from one fund to another without additional charges.

Management Fees
Keep an eye on management fees. They can make or break an investment. Funds
are characterized as "load" or "no load" funds. Depending on how long you plan on
holding the funds, they can be more or less attractive.

- **"No Load"**
  These funds don't charge fees in advance or on redemption. They charge, however,
  during the term or for other services.

- **"Load"**
  These funds charge up front when you buy and/or have a redemption fee when
  you sell. These funds give you a choice of an up-front sales charge, a redemption
  fee or an annual fee. Both have internal charges whether loaded or not. Keep
  in mind that just because the fund may or may not have a load doesn't mean
  the performance will be better or worse. Consulting an expert is always a
  good thing.

Tax Consequences

Most mutual funds will send you a 1099 DIV at the end of the year for any capital gains realized. This may create a taxable event for you. You may want to check the fund's capital gains experience. Some funds create a situation where you can receive a taxable gain without receiving a cash distribution, thus, you can end up paying taxes on money that you don't even receive. Check out the timing of distributions when buying.

Types Of Funds

There are various types of funds, which vary in size, category, and investment goals. Some are focused on particular industries such as electronics, gold, or foreign funds. Others vary their investment categories. Major categories include income funds, growth funds, growth and income funds, global funds, and international funds.

Research

Make sure you research before buying a mutual fund. You can find out many details on the internet and through brokers. Also, check out papers, such as Barron's and The Wall Street Journal, and magazines, such as Fortune and Money.

HELPFUL WEB SITES

- www.morningstar.com
- www.cnnfn.com
- http://sec.gov/info/advisers.shtml
- www.scottrade.com/frame_mutualfunds.asp
- www.www.ici.org/funds/inv/bro_understanding_mfs.html

IRA's

No, we're not talking about the your Uncle Ira, although I could go for one of his old jokes about now. This section will help you start to plan for your future, so pay attention.

Definition
"IRA" stands for "Individual Retirement Account."

Types
There are 3 basic types of IRA's: 1) traditional IRA, 2) Roth IRA, and 3) SEP IRA's for self-employed persons.

Traditional IRA's And SEP IRA's
Contributions are tax deductible (up to certain limits), the earnings are tax-deferred, and distributions are fully taxable. There are complicated rules that change frequently, so talk with a qualified individual when creating an IRA and making later contributions.

Roth IRA's
Contributions are non-deductible, earnings accumulate tax-free, and distributions are tax-free. Money in a Roth IRA can be withdrawn without penalties for such reasons as education and house payments. If withdrawn for any other reason before reaching age 59 1/2, you would be penalized 10% of the withdrawal amount and also subject to ordinary income tax.

Funding
Remember to fund your IRA on a consistent basis, based on the maximum contribution that you can make and how much you can afford to deposit. Consult IRS rules and investment/tax advisors on an annual basis to determine the right amount for you.

Who Holds My IRA?
Choose a reputable and helpful financial company that can provide services at a reasonable rate; these can include banks, brokerage companies, or mutual fund companies.

What Can I Put In My IRA?
IRA's can include stocks, bonds, mutual funds, or various other investments.

> " It is the secret of the world that all things subsist and do not die, but only retire from sight and afterwards return again. "
>
> Josh Billings

HELPFUL WEB SITES
- www.fairmark.com/rothira
- http://taxes.yahoo.com/guide/rothira
- www.ira.com
- www.smartmoney.com/retirement/roth/index.cfm?story=whichira

STUFF & SKILLS
FOR MY CASA
(and a little entertaining thrown in)

section
05

How To Buy Art & Still Afford To Eat

Buying art does not always have to be costly. Here are several suggestions for purchasing original, inexpensive art while on a budget. Who knows...if you invest wisely, you could even turn a profit.

The Most Important Thing To Keep In Mind...
Purchasing a work of art is not only an investment in a tangible item, it is an investment in the artist's potential to continue to make great work. For this reason, it is important to assess both the art and the artist before making a purchase.

What to Look For When Buying Art

- **Do you love the artwork?** This question may seem silly and subjective, but the truth is... if you do not love it, do not buy it. Your taste is one of the best judgment tools you have at your disposal. As your taste changes, you can always think about upgrading your collection. Your daily return on investment will be the pleasure you receive from living with the work.

- **Is the item well crafted and in prime condition?** You do not want to purchase something that will soon fall apart or crack. Inspect the front and back of a painting. The stretcher bars should feel strong and supportive, sturdy and straight. Corners should seem square. Beware of warped canvases that do not hang flush against a wall. Works on paper must be framed under glass in order to avoid damage from natural elements (dirt, sun, etc.)

- **Does the artist seem self-disciplined and dedicated to his/her work?** You will want to purchase from an artist who seems most likely to continue to learn and make quality work, not one who lacks passion and dedication. If the artist is both talented and headstrong when it comes to making and promoting art, then he/she will probably be successful at selling work and finding exhibition opportunities. The more work an artist sells and the more exhibition opportunities the artist has, the greater the value of that artist's work. You will want to find an artist who is full of potential and professional promise.

How Art Is Priced
Art is typically priced according to its quality, its size, its materials, the artist's experience/exhibition history, and the artist's past sales. You should ask if the artist has sold work in the past. If so, the quoted price you are given should fit within a close range of that artist's recent sales (assuming those recent sales were for works of similar dimensions and materials). Before you ask for the price, assign an approximate value in your head for what you would pay for the piece. If the work is not in a gallery setting, it may help to picture the work in an art gallery. Use the imaginary gallery

price as the maximum price you would pay for that work. Then ask the artist (or whoever is selling the work) what the actual price is. If your estimate and the actual price are not too far off, then you may want to consider purchasing the work.

Best Places To Find Inexpensive, Original Artwork

- **Attend college art exhibits:** By going to an exhibit featuring undergraduate or graduate students, you will see fresh, up-and-coming artwork, usually at undervalued prices. Most students are hoping to sell work at these shows, even if you do not see prices. If you see something you like, express interest. Leave your phone number or email address in case the artist is not available or is not ready to make an immediate decision. If you do not know who the artist is, then mention your interest to one of the faculty members in charge. At the very least, the artist will be flattered by your interest.

- **Consider browsing through art studios the next time you are on a college campus:** Be respectful and do not touch anything! Just look. If you see something you like, leave a note with your contact information. It would be wise to check with the art department before wandering around school property unannounced.

- **Try to buy art directly from artists who are not yet affiliated with galleries:** Be one of the first people to discover an emerging artist's talent. As any artist will tell you, there are many more talented artists than galleries. The ideal, most profitable situation, would be to buy from an artist who is on the verge of being discovered by a reputable gallery. Chances are that the artist's work will only increase in value once a gallery jumps onboard. Galleries not only establish the retail prices of artwork, they provide opportunities (such as exhibitions and sales) that help increase retail values. Galleries also publicly promote the artist, helping the artist gain exposure. Buying early might be a wise investment as many young, undiscovered artists underestimate the monetary values of their work. Most of these young, undiscovered artists lack confidence in setting high (or even fair) prices. Galleries, on the other hand, have no trouble recognizing the full values of artworks. In fact, some galleries may even overvalue works of art so that they can afford to discount professional art consultants and loyal clientele. Once an artist becomes officially affiliated with a gallery, all sales are supposed to go through the gallery and not the artist. At this time the prices may rise in order for both the gallery and the artist to make a profit.

- **The internet, as well as local newspapers:** Artists often have their own websites and sometimes also place ads in local art publications. Look for these free art newspapers on street corners, restaurants, and art supply stores. If you find an artist of interest, contact him/her and possibly set up a studio visit. This approach is also a good way to explore art in each new city you visit.

- **Local artist communities:** Most cities have at least one building dedicated to artist studios. Artists rent out workspaces in these buildings and, typically, hold special events once a month. These art openings are open to the public, and usually most work is for sale.

- **Local art clubs and societies:** These organizations put on public exhibitions at least once a year. Usually, artists affiliated with art clubs and societies do not have gallery representation. Remember, gallery representation usually means higher prices.

- **Summer fairs:** Not only are art fairs a fun thing to do on a sunny day, but you will probably see many varieties of art to help you narrow your preferences. Be aware that not all art fairs display quality artwork.

> *" Art is not a treasure in the past or an importation from another land, but part of the present life of all living and creating peoples. "*

Franklin D. Roosevelt

HELPFUL WEB SITES

- www.artfair.org
- www.saintlouisartfair.com
- http://scadexhibitions.com
- http://risd.edu/exhibitions.cfm
- www.art.com

Furnishing Your Apartment

Now that you're on your way to a futon-less place, you should begin your search for furniture. Required fall move-ins and compulsory spring moveouts are a thing of the past, so you don't have to narrow your search to pieces that you move twice a year.

Plan
Before you begin buying furniture, walk around your new place and sketch out a room layout or room design. Think about where you want to have each piece.

Take Inventory
Compile a list of furniture and pictures that you already have, or those that your parents/grandparents/siblings will give you.

Get A Deal
Make sure you shop around if you're in the market for new furniture. Ask your sales people if the pieces will go on sale soon, if they have any floor or scratched/dented models, when they change over their inventory and therefore would be more likely to deal, and if they have any packaged pieces of furniture.

Credit Cards
Some stores give you a percentage off of your purchase when you sign up for their credit card. So, plan your purchases and try to use this extra percentage off. Think about it, if you're spending $1,000 on furniture you may save $100 for just getting a credit card.

Moving And Assembly
Take into account the weight and dimension of each piece and who will assemble them. Don't forget to ask how much assembly and delivery will be.

Buying Used
You may want to hit flea markets, garage sales, online liquidators or classified sales in the newspaper if you like the challenge of rooting out a bargain or uncovering an antique treasure. Also, search for students who are moving out of town. They may just want to get rid of their stuff, and might take any offer.

Make Your Own
Sometime you can improvise in furnishing your place. Think about making your own desk out of a door and two filing cabinets, or building shelves out of cut plywood and brackets.

> *" Books are not made for furniture, but there is nothing else that so beautifully furnishes a house. "*
>
> Henry Ward Beecher

HELPFUL WEB SITES

- www.ikea.com
- www.buy-slipcovers.com
- www.hermanmiller.com
- www.furniture.com
- www.interfaceflor.com
- www.dwr.com

Buying A Computer

Is your 1GB hard drive filled up with MP3's, and does it take 3 minutes to get a web page up on your computer? Maybe it's time to transition into a new machine with your move into working life. Here are some terms to become familiar with and things to look for.

Laptop vs. Desktop

What will you be doing with the machine? Do you want to take it with you on the plane, or from work to home? Do you just want something to check your email and listen to music on? Also, consider what your computer situation is at work - will they be giving you a laptop? Think about if you want this to be a performance machine that is fast, or if you want something cheaper and portable. You may also consider a tablet PC that allows you to write on the screen.

Platform

You probably are already dedicated to a PC or a Mac at this point, but if you were thinking of switching, now may be a good time to do so. Consider what external devices you have or want (ie. printers, scanners, digital cameras, MP3 players, etc.) and their compatibility. Also, think about the programs you want to install on your machine, and if they will work on your new machine.

Brand

This is sometimes a tough choice. The brand of your computer comes into question usually when you have customer service issues. A good way to determine companies that treat customers well is to ask around. Ask your friends if they've had good luck with their computer and its service. It's more than likely you will get at least one war story. Also, check out magazine and online reviews.

Pricing

You likely know how much you want to spend on your machine, so work around that. Computers get cheaper and cheaper by the day. If you're content with a model that is not the newest on the market, you can probably get a good deal. Also, shop around, both online and in stores. Remember, you can save sales tax by ordering on the internet, which is a big savings on a purchase of $500 plus.

Get A Deal

Consider buying a refurbished machine from the manufacturer or from an online auction company if you want to save some money. These are computers that have been returned and inspected by the company. Usually they have a warranty and are much cheaper than brand-new machines. Also, see if any companies give student discounts, alumni discounts, organizational discounts, etc.

Warranty

Your warranty can be a major issue down the road. Compare the coverage different manufacturers offer. Will they come to your house? How long do they cover the machine? What do they cover? Also, find out if purchasing with certain credit cards extends your warranty.

Terms

Here are some terms to know and think about when shopping:

- **Hard Drive**
  The size of storage on the computer for files, programs, music, video, etc. This is identified in terms of Gigabytes (GB) and most machines start at 40 GB.

- **Memory**
  The amount of temporary memory your computer can use when it is turned on (RAM). This allows the computer to quickly grab information, and affects how fast programs load and process requests. Most new computers contain around 256 Megs of RAM. If you'll be running only a few lightweight programs, you can do just fine with 128. For heavier loads, 512 and even a Gig of RAM is recommended.

- **Processor**
  This is what does the actual calculations and "thinking" for your machine. New machines come with processing speeds above a gigahertz, though you can get them with more if needed.

- **CD-R/DVD-R**
  Used for burning CDs and DVDs. Speeds on these range from 8x to 52x; The slower, more affordable burners work just as well as the faster models, if you don't mind waiting longer for your burns to complete.

- **Modems/Ethernet**
  Your gateway to the internet. Most people in the US have switched over to high-speed internet connections, leaving their dial up modems in the dust. With the use of cable modems, DSL and other broadband options, fast connections are the preferred option in a new machine. High speed connections (Ethernet) are usually provided as the default option in new computers, but it might be worth the upgrade if this is not the case with the machine you are considering, unless you don't mind slower downloads. More and more people are using wireless networks at home and at work, so check to see if your computer has wireless capabilities installed, or what it would cost to get your computer wireless.

Screens

What type of monitor do you want with your machine? If you're going to be spending a lot of time at the computer, consider getting a bigger screen as it will be easier to read. If you don't use it that much, think about getting a cheap one. Weigh getting a smaller flat screen monitor vs. a larger full monitor.

> *"Home computers are being called upon to perform many new functions, including the consumption of homework formely eaten by the dog."*
>
> Doug Larson

HELPFUL WEB SITES

- http://reviews.cnet.com/2001-1_7-0.html?legacy=cnet
- www.pcmag.com/category2/0,4148,22,00.asp
- www.dell.com
- www.gateway.com
- www.apple.com
- www.dellauction.com
- www.toshibadirect.com/td/b2c/home.to

Securing Your Computer Network

So, you've now got a wicked awesome network, but you're worried someone may be viewing all those fan emails you send to your favorite boy band? The answer to save face and make sure those emails get there in one piece is to secure your network. While the following may get a little technical, it will allow you have some terms to discuss with computer savvy friends or technicians.

Overview

Security is commonly addressed in layers: 1) your broadband connection coming in from your DSL, cable modem, or satellite, 2) your home network after your broadband connection, and 3) the computers on your home network.

Secure Your Broadband Connection

Securing your broadband connection is the easiest, so long as you have the right hardware. Most equipment available has a built-in firewall and NAT device, and some have more advanced features. A firewall prevents unwanted or unauthorized data from entering your home network from your broadband connection. A NAT device disguises your home network from the perspective of your broadband connection, making it difficult for attackers to determine what devices you have on your home network. These two features are usually enabled by default with the correct settings on most home equipment. Finally, some devices have more advanced features, such as filters that will not permit users on your home network to visit websites with keywords you choose.

Secure Your Home Network

- Once you have secured your broadband connection, you need to secure your home network. For a wired network, such as Ethernet, this is a minor issue, as it is easy to control the location of your network cables. With wireless networks you have to worry about who has access to that network. Three common tools available on most modern wireless access points include Wired Equivalent Privacy (WEP), MAC filtering, and Wireless Protected Access (WPA).

- Each network card is assigned a unique number at the factory, called the MAC address. Most home access points can restrict usage to the wireless network to only network cards with MAC addresses you allow. Though this security measure can be easily circumvented, it does provide an additional layer of security.

- Think of WEP as a password for your wireless network. No machine can use your wireless network without your WEP password, and WEP also provides encryption for all the data traveling over your wireless network. Though some security concerns surround WEP and the fact that it is possible for attackers to discover the WEP key, it is not a trivial process, and WEP will likely provide adequate security for a home network.

- WPA is the next level of WEP. Like WEP it encrypts data on your wireless network, and requires users to enter a password to use your wireless network. WPA does not have the same security concerns of WEP, though it does require compatible hardware and software.

Secure Your Computer

The final step is to secure each computer on your home network. There are several basic steps you should perform on each computer to properly safeguard it against security threats:

- Make certain your computer has a password enabled, and make certain it is not a simple password such as "password", "blank", or your username. Good passwords consist of letters and numbers, upper case and lower case, and special characters such as "!@#$%".

- Make sure your machine is current on all recent patches. This can be done easily in Microsoft by visiting www.windowsupdate.com, or by using the Windows Update feature included in XP. For other operating systems check with your manufacturer.

- Install a personal firewall on each computer. This is an additional firewall to the one on your residential gateway or DSL router. This provides an additional layer of security and prevents attackers who gain access to your network from gaining further access to your PC. If you have a laptop, this also protects your computer when you travel away from the security of your home network. Popular firewalls include Symantec, Tiny, and ZoneAlarm. Windows XP also has a built-in firewall, but it is not enabled by default.

- Install and maintain updated antivirus software. Many vendors offer good antivirus software, such as Symantec and McAfee. Most computers come with trial antivirus software, and if you like it, you should consider buying a subscription. Note that most antivirus software requires a subscription, and usually requires to be renewed annually. Antivirus software today is so common that most vendors will provide adequate protection. Some vendors may include additional features, such as firewalls or intrusion detection systems within their products.

HELPFUL WEB SITES

- www.pandasoftware.com
- www.windowsupdate.com
- www.symantec.com
- www.macafee.com
- www.specialopssecurity.com

Choosing And Setting Up
Your Internet Connection

Most academic environments provided you with a reliable, secure, and fast connection to the internet. Now, you have moved out of the dorms, away from your geek friends who set up your computer, and no longer have the university wireless system to roam about freely with your laptop. Would you like to have these things back, but don't know where to start?

Getting Connected

You get what you pay for, and the price-conscious market of choosing an Internet Service Provider (ISP) is no exception. Speed, price, and availability are the three key factors used in selecting your ISP.

- **Dial Up**

  Modems allow data transfer over phone lines, and it's the phone technology that limits data transfer to 56Kbps. Chances are your computer has a modem and you will not have to buy any additional equipment. No dial-up connection should cost over $30/month, with the average around $15/month. If you plan to do anything more than send email, don't get a dial-up, go for one of the options below.

- **Cable vs. Digital Subscriber Line (DSL)**

  - Cable modems and DSL are the two most common broadband solutions in America today. Cable modems rely on the same cables you use for cable TV, and tend to be available in more locations. DSL requires special equipment to be installed by your phone company, and you must be within 15,000 feet of this equipment.

  - Price is about the same between the two, though a cable modem is generally cheaper by the bit. The price of your DSL connection varies based on your speed, while a cable modem usually only comes at one speed and that's what you pay for. Shop around for prices, and some cable or phone companies will provide you a package deal if you buy multiple services.

  - Both technologies can download faster than they upload, so if you plan to use this technology to run a server do not expect great performance. Cable modems tend to be faster during off-peak hours, because the line is shared with others in your area. DSL is more expensive per Mbit, but will provide you with a consistent speed.

  - If you are security-conscious, choose a DSL connection if possible. Cable modems share a connection with others on your street, so your neighbors get your data and vice versa. Any tech-savvy person can intercept the data and view it. DSL on the other hand is a dedicated line for you.

- Reliability depends on two things, the networking equipment and the transmission lines. Both have comparable network equipment, though a cable modem does slow down and sometimes become unusable during extreme peak times. Consider your local phone and cable company, which do you trust more to keep your lines up and running?

- Remember that cable modems and DSL still require an ISP to log in to and connect to the internet. They also require either a DSL modem or cable modem, both of which are usually provided for you to rent or buy; if you buy your own, you may receive additional features that the stock modem won't have. DSL and cable companies usually provide the ISP, and your connection will appear seamless.

	Cable Modem	DSL
Price	$40/mo.	$40/mo. (varies with speed)
Speed	Faster than DSL during off peak, slower during peak hours	Consistent speed, though slower than cable
Availability	1.5Mb DL 128UL	385 DL 128 UL (and higher)
Security	Shared connection with neighbors	Dedicated connection for you
Reliability	How often does your cable go out?	How often does your phone line go out?

- **Satellite**
  Satellite is a means of last resort for those too remote for wireless, DSL, or cable, but cannot stand a dial-up connection. It is usually more expensive than cable or DSL, but can provide faster download speeds than an average DSL package. Upload speeds tend to be much slower than DSL or Cable, and satellite has a latency issue, due to the time it takes the signal to travel to the satellite and back to earth.

Setting Up Your Home Network

So you have your ISP decided, and you have one computer in your house or apartment. As a recent college graduate, chances are you won't be living alone and will have to share your broadband with your roommates. You really only have two choices here, wired, which will give you more privacy, higher speeds, and lower costs, or wireless, which allows for mobility. Both allow you to connect multiple computers to one broadband connection and use that connection at the same time. They also provide basic security features you should have on any broadband connection.

Wired

Almost all modern wired home networks will be set up using Ethernet and CAT 5 cabling. The simplest network is to buy a residential gateway, Cable/DSL router, or similar device that allows you to connect to your broadband modem. They will cost about $50 and can be found at almost any electronic store. Do not use a hub to connect your computer to the broadband modem, as you will leave your computer open to attack from the internet unless you take other appropriate precautions. You also need cables to connect your computers to the router, which you can purchase in any length, usually up to 100 feet. Finally you need a network card, which comes with most modern computers.

Wireless

- If you are setting up network from scratch, go wireless. It CAN be secured properly for a home user, though it takes a little more effort, and if you use a laptop it will be well worth the investment. You can purchase a residential gateway or Cable/DSL router with additional wireless capability ($100), or you can add it to an existing gateway or router with a wireless access point ($75). You also need a wireless network card for each computer on the network ($60). Some newer laptops have them built in, so check your laptop before you buy.

- Wireless for home networking uses the 802.11 standard, and several standards have emerged for wireless, with more on the way. The original usable standard was 802.11b, which transfers data at 11Mbit. This is a very usable speed for most applications and has a range of about 150 feet in your average home, depending on walls, power lines, materials and other factors. 802.11b operates in the 2.4Ghz range, which may suffer from interference from microwave ovens and 2.4Ghz phones. Standards more recently on the market include 802.11a, which has a higher bandwidth than 802.11b, shorter range, and operates on a different frequency of 5Ghz. 802.11g is the latest to market, which combines the best of both. Operating at 2.4Ghz, 802.11g provides the range of 802.11b with the speeds of 802.11a. Before you get confused with the different standards, evaluate them like this - if you are on a budget, go with 802.11b, if you're not, go with 802.11g. 802.11a has become usurped by 802.11g, and is outdated in the marketplace for most applications.

- The primary danger of home wireless networks is that wireless signals go beyond the walls of your home or apartment. Signals can easily penetrate to your neighbors or public spaces, such as the street, patios, lounges, or nearby parks. This is a security concern because you will be freely sharing your internet access with your neighbors. The impact may be as minimal as consuming your bandwidth, to as much as performing illegal activities from your internet. Of a lesser concern to home users is that your data may be traveling across the airwaves in an unencrypted form, which may be easily read by other users on your wireless network.

On The Road

If you travel a lot think about purchasing a wireless account that you can access from stores, restaurants, hotels, and other locations throughout the country. These can range in price from $10/day to $40/month, but can be great when you need to check email at 10:35 p.m. when you're traveling in New Mexico.

> "You see, wire telegraph is a kind of a very, very long cat. You pull his tail in New York and his head is meowing in Los Angeles. Do you understand this? And Radio operates exactly the same way: you send signals here, they receive them there. The only difference is that there is no cat. "

Albert Einstein,
when asked to describe radio

HELPFUL WEB SITES

- www.wi-fiplanet.com
- www.windowsupdate.com
- www.cnet.com/4520-7363_1-6361076-1.html
- http://hotspot.t-mobile.com
- www.linksys.com
- www.dslreports.com

How To Buy A Stereo Or Home Entertainment System

A little education is essential if you're going to make the kind of investment that will "rock the house." Combat the salesperson's hard sell by reviewing these suggestions.

What You'll Need:

In addition to a TV, you'll need a receiver and speakers. A receiver integrates a preamplifier (which is what you plug your DVD player, VCR, CD player, etc., into) and powered amplifier (which drives the speakers) into one box. It's the central hub of any home theater or stereo system. Prices range from $200 to well over $10,000.

What Will You Use It For?

If you're only listening to music, get a basic stereo receiver with only two amplified channels. If you want to watch DVDs in surround sound, get a home theater receiver with at least five applied channels.

What Is "5.1"?

Most receivers are labeled "5.1 Surround Sound." This simply means that they can power five speakers (the "5") and have a subwoofer output (the ".1").

Surround Formats

To play surround sound DVDs, a receiver must be able to process the digital sound format, so make sure that a home theater receiver can process Dolby Digital and DTS sound. Steer clear of those labeled "Dolby Digital Ready" because you will need to buy a separate Dolby Digital processor.

Watts

If you're buying a home theater receiver, you'll probably want one that can send 100 watts to each of its five channels. Look for more power if you have a larger room.

Number Of Inputs On The Receiver

How many devices are you going to hook up to your receiver? Make sure the receiver has enough inputs for all of your audio/video devices, and has extras in case your system grows. A minimum of five inputs is recommended.

Type Of Inputs

In a home theater receiver, make sure that every video channel has at least an S-Video and a composite (RCA) input. You'll also want at least one or two component inputs, especially if you have a newer TV, or are planning to get one. On the audio side, look for an ample number of digital inputs; both optical and coaxial are necessary if you want digital surround sound. If you want to future-proof your system (and spend extra cash), you might also look for FireWire (IEEE 1394), DVI, Ethernet, and USB connections.

Build Quality
Good equipment has a quality feel to it. Receivers will be made of metal and speakers will have solid wood cabinets, not plastic. Good components are heavy. Also look for binding posts that screw down on your speaker cables on both the receiver and the speakers; cheaper models will cut corners with "spring clips" that just bite down on the wires.

Pre-Outs And Multi-Channel Inputs
These won't be available on entry-level units, but they're good to have. A set of pre-outs will let you use your receiver with a separate power amplifier if you ever decide you need more power. Multi-channel inputs (or "5.1-channel inputs") are a good future-proofing feature, and are necessary if you plan on using the emerging DVD Audio or Super Audio CD (SACD) formats.

Don't Get Fooled
Most receivers have many different sound "processing" modes, such as Hall, Acoustic, Live, Action, etc. These are gimmicky and often worthless. Don't base your decision on them.

Your Speakers
If you're only listening to music, you only need two speakers, but if you want surround sound, you'll need at least five (Left, Right, Center, Surround Right, Surround Left) and a powered subwoofer. Be sure to buy all one brand; different manufacturer's speakers have different timbres, so mixing and matching will make your system sound disoriented.

Get Big Speakers
Larger speakers move more air, thus, creating a larger, fuller sound. No matter what anyone tells you, those tiny (and often overpriced) cube speakers that fit in your hand won't give you good performance. If you have special or aesthetic limitations, many companies make good-sounding bookshelf speakers; just be sure to pair them with a good subwoofer, as most won't produce lower bass frequencies.

Powered Subwoofers

Subs aren't essential, but they are what give a home theater system its "rumble." It has its own built-in powered amplifier, so look for one in the 100-150 watt range (more if you have a larger room).

Listen

Speaker preference varies wildly by individual. Try to find a dealer who will let you take a sample pair home to try out.

Do Your Homework

Research what you're buying before you buy. Internet forums are a great way to get loads of free, unbiased information about any gear.

> **"** *I don't know anything about music. In my line you don't have to.* **"**
>
> Elvis Presley

HELPFUL WEB SITES

- www.hometheaterforum.com
- reviews-zdnet.com.com/4520-7298_16-4207839.html
- www.epinions.com/elec?tab=1

Buying Or Renting A Washer & Dryer

Have your friends come to the conclusion that you've taken up painting with food and all your clothes are smocks? You need clean clothes, right? It is much more convenient to have a washer/dryer in your place, so here are some things to keep in mind.

Measure Your Space
You don't want to get the units up six flights of stairs only to find out they do not fit. Also, note whether your place is set up to hold a stacking washer/dryer or a traditional side-by-side model.

Gas Or Electric
Check your outlets before you head to the store. Also, consider your intended length of stay at your current location, and whether gas or electric is the norm for the area where you want to move.

Size Of The Machine
The dryer will need to be one size larger than the washer. Also, the smaller the washing machine, the smaller the loads, resulting in more washings and more water used, which means higher water bills.

Basket Type
Plastic drum, porcelain paint on a steel drum or speckled porcelain paint on a steel drum? Plastic drums won't rust, but are less durable than steel. The fully porcelain painted steel drums are durable and will prevent rusting better than the speckled porcelain drums, but are more expensive.

Renting
Hassle free, but you will spend more in the long run than if you buy. Rental companies will install and maintain units for a monthly fee.

Buying Used
If you are not picky, you should be able to find a decent pair. You'll likely be picking up and installing them yourself. Remember, some people would rather sell a washer and dryer than move them, especially if they are moving into a smaller place. So check out bulletin boards for deals. Also, ask friends and relatives - some may want to upgrade and sell their old machines.

Buying Scratch And Dent

Department/appliance stores will offer cheaper prices for units that have scratches or dents. Often times, the scratches and dents are not noticeable or are located on the sides that are not visible when the unit is in place. Who really looks at your washer or dryer anyway?

Buying Brand New

Buying brand new will give you the most options, but first you must try to decide on the features you want. Go to a couple of appliance stores and ask the salespeople a lot of questions. Do I need a delicate cycle? Auto moisture sensing? Auto dry? Three water temperatures? Permanent press? Once you have found a washer/dryer that you like, watch for a couple of weeks for sales, or other incentives such as free shipping, free installation or zero interest financing.

HELPFUL WEB SITES

- www.sears.com
- www.ianr.unl.edu/pubs/housing/nf346.htm
- www.diynetwork.com/diy/diy_kits/article/0,2019,DIY_13787_2847575,00.html
- www.craigslist.com
- http://ianrpubs.unl.edu/housing/nf348.htm

Digital Cameras And Photography

You think that archiving your "crazy" Halloween Party is a good idea, but cleaning up your trashed place takes precedence over film development. Solution: a digital camera. Check out the info below to be better prepared in choosing the right camera.

Price

Cost is usually a key. Think about how much you want to spend, how long you plan to use the camera and how often you take pictures now. Prices range from under $100 into the thousands.

Type

The two kinds that should be considered are point-and-shoot digital cameras and digital Single Lens Reflex (SLR) cameras. Most amateurs prefer the point-and-shoot due to its simplicity and user friendliness. Photographic enthusiasts like the digital SLR camera, which provides more control over the camera settings (focus, F-stop, lens interchangeability, etc.).

Memory

Photo quality and the number of photos you can store in a camera depends on memory card size. There are various types of media formats, including CompactFlash and Smartmedia. Think about other products you own that have such media cards. Also, consider which formats are popular, the expense of extra media, and how many pictures, and at what quality, each card holds.

Resolution

The size and quality of your picture will depend on the resolution setting you choose on the camera. Think about what you want to do with your pictures before you check out cameras. Do you want to blow them up for a poster, share them on the internet, or print them out? Your end goal will determine what resolution you should use. Typically, a 3 megapixel camera will be able to provide images for posting to a website or emailing to friends; however, if you will be printing them out as 8"X10" images or larger, a 4 megapixel or greater camera is recommended.

Print Size	Min. Image Resolution Req.
4 x 6	900 x 800 pixels
5 x 7	1050 x 750 pixels
8 x 10	1280 x 1024 pixels

Batteries

Consider the battery life in your camera, the charge time of your batteries, the price of extra batteries, and the life of such batteries. Also, think about the cost of AC adapters and whether one is included with the camera.

Zoom

Check out cameras with various types of zoom, both physical and digital. Many cameras may have a small physical zoom with a large digital zoom to keep their size down. While this can come in handy, digital zooms don't offer the same quality as physical zooms.

LCD Screen

Some cameras have little LCD screens on the back so you can get instant feedback and delete the bad pictures immediately. Such screens are great, but take up battery life, so take that into consideration.

Transferring

How are you going to get the pictures onto a computer or to a printer? Is a cable included? Do you have to buy a card reader for your storage media? What types of connections on your computer are necessary (USB, FireWire, serial ports, etc.) What is the speed of transferring pictures? Do you own or want to purchase a printer that connects directly to your camera, so that you can print out your pictures directly?

Your Computer

Don't forget compatibility with your computer. Think about its connections, your free hard drive space, cd/dvd writing ability, and your operating system.

Storage

Pictures can take up a lot of room on your camera and hard drive, so think about how you're going to store them (online?, on cds?, on dvd's?, etc.).

Sharing

What do you want to do with your pictures? Will you print a lot? If so, think about buying a photo printer. Will you share them through an online service? If so, think about printing costs, online software, and storage sizes of your account.

HELPFUL WEB SITES

- www.pcphotoreview.com
- www.snapfish.com
- www.kodakgallery.com
- www.hp.com/you
- www.shutterfly.com
- www.flickr.com
- http://reviews.cnet.com/Digital_cameras/2001-6501_7-0.html?tag=cnetfd.dir

All About MP3's

So you thought your parents were the only people whose music media would become outdated? You were wrong. Your expansive CD collection that used to take half your closet now can fit in the palm of your hand. MP3's are the growing music medium, and there is no better time than now to jump on the bandwagon.

What Is An MP3?
An MP3 is an audio file that is compressed by a computer. A good rule is that a minute of music will take up one megabyte of data.

Where Can I Get MP3's?
* There are several web sites where you can pay MP3's, such as iTunes.com or Buymusic.com. At these sites you can pick and choose songs and even buy the whole album if you choose.

* When choosing a download service think about limits on burning and sharing of the songs. Compare prices between legal downloading sites. Some MP3 sites may not offer all albums.

* You can even create your own MP3's using such software as MusicMatch or iTunes. Such software may be prepackaged with your computer, or they can be downloaded. With such programs, you can rip your cd collection into MP3's and store them on your computer. Remember, that CD quality is 128 kbps.

How Do I Play MP3's?

* **On your computer**
  You can play MP3's on your computer through an audio program such as Window's Media Player, MusicMatch or iTunes. Most computers come with an audio program that will play MP3's.

* **On your MP3 player**
  You can purchase an MP3 player, which is essentially a mini hard drive that you can take with you. You download songs from your computer onto the player and can have hours of music on your player to take with you.

* **On your CD/DVD player**
  Many CD/DVD players will play data discs that contain MP3's on them. You can store hundreds of songs in MP3 format on a CD-R, and if your player allows it, you can play it through your stereo/audio-visual system.

Buying An MP3 Player

- **Decide what you want to use it for**
  Will it be for commuting on the subway, will it be for sitting at your desk with a headset on, or will it be for working out. Depending on your use you will want to look at the durability/waterproofing of the unit. Also think about buying multitasking machines, like PDA's or cell phones that can play music.

- **Decide how much you want to spend**
  It will be $300 or more if you want the top of the line player that can hold your entire music collection. Cheaper players can be purchased for below $100.

- **Decide how much music you want to have**
  If you just want to use it for a 30-minute run three times a week, then you won't need a 10-gigabyte player; maybe a 64-megabyte unit will do (remember a megabyte is about 1 minute of music). If you will be taking long trips think about a player with much more storage capacity.

- **Think about audio software you like using**
  Consider the compatibility between the software you like, your computer, and the MP3 player.

- **What other types of features do you want?**
  Do you want something that you can wear on your arm while you run, something that has a built in radio, something that can act as a multimedia device (also playing videos and games) or something that can broadcast on an FM frequency so that you can play it through your car or home stereo?

HELPFUL WEB SITES

- www.imusic.com
- www.buymusic.com
- www.musicmatch.com
- www.itunes.com
- www.ipod.com
- www.dell.com
- www.napster.com
- http://reviews.cnet.com/Music/2001-6450_7-0.html
- www1.us.dell.com/content/products/category.aspx/dj?c=us&cs=19&l=en&s=dhs

First Aid For Your Home

Did your parents want you to become a doctor, but the thought of all those years of schooling made you shutter? Well, you don't need much schooling to pinch-hit in an emergency situation. Here are some preparations everyone should make.

First Aid Kit
Include the following items, amongst others, for your kit.

- Latex/Sterile Gloves - 2 pairs
- Bandages- various sizes
- Ointments- antibiotic (prevents infections) and burn
- Antihistamine Creams - for rashes, bug bites and allergic reactions
- First aid tape
- Gauze
- Scissors - to cut bandages and gauze
- Cotton Swabs (keep clean in a bag or container)
- Tweezers - to remove splinters
- Calamine - for poison ivy, chicken pox, other rashes
- Rubbing Alcohol
- Thermometer

Medications To Have
While you might hate swallowing pills or are always as healthy as an ox, you should have general medications on hand for you or your guests in case of an emergency.

- Aspirin/Non-Aspirin pain reliever
- Anti-diarrhea medicine
- Syrup of Ipecac - use if advised to by Poison Control Center
- Laxatives
- Activated Charcoal- use if advised to by Poison Control Center
- Antacids

Lifesaving Skills

CPR
Cardiopulmonary Resuscitation is a skill everyone should learn. Classes are usually taught at hospitals, community centers, or schools, so make sure you take one. In an emergency, though, here are some quick reminders.

- Check the victim, if victim is unresponsive, call 911.
- Remember A, B, C's

  A - Airway: Open the airway with the head tilt-chin lift maneuver or jaw thrust

  B - Breathing: Look, listen and feel for signs of breathing

  C - Circulation: Check for signs of circulation
- Pump and Blow: Cycles of 15 compressions and 2 rescue breaths (for adults)

Choking

- The Heimlich maneuver needs to be performed with permission if the victim is conscious, is in distress, has an ineffective cough and is over 1 year old.
- If the adult victim becomes unresponsive, phone 911 and then attempt CPR (above) For infants and children, give 20 cycles of CPR before calling 911.

HELPFUL WEB SITES

- www.my.webmd.com
- www.redcross.org
- www.aapcc.org
- www.americanheart.org

Wine Stuff

Don't let them dazzle you with wine snobbery. Wine is a great drink for your health and a great complement to food. So, take the plunge and learn a little bit about how itty-bitty grapes form a classic and classy drink.

What Is Wine?
Wine is the fermented juice of grapes. Yeast transforms the sugar in the grapes into alcohol. There are variations of wines made with other fruits, but as a rule "real wine" is made from grapes. Champagne is also made from grapes; it is a sparkling white wine.

Red Wine
The color in red wine comes from grape skins, grape seeds, and stems, which gives it both a darker color and, usually, a bolder taste than white wine. There are various types of red wines including:

- **Pinot Noir**
  One of the most renowned red grapes for its versatility with food, supple texture and earthy yet bold berry and fruit flavors.

- **Zinfandel**
  The red varietal is fermented with the grape skins, while the white is not. This makes the white one of the lightest bodied wines with the red having a full body texture.

- **Cabernet**
  This famous full-bodied Bordeaux wine, often called the "king of grapes," is a powerful wine with a distinct blackberry aroma and juicy plum, currant, and deep rich cassis flavors.

- **Syrah**
  This Rhone Valley wine is called Shiraz in Australia and has spicy - particularly white pepper - smoky, floral, and berry fruit notes.

- **Merlot**
  Often blended with Cabernet, it is less tannic and softer on the palate. It has huge chocolate notes, with vanilla, toffee, and cherry flavors.

- **Burgundy**
  With the exception of Beaujolais, red Burgundy wines made in France are made from pinot noir grapes. The white Burgundy wines are made from the Chardonnay grape.

White Wine

While the grapes may be the same as those used in red wines, white wines do not include the skins, seeds, or stems. Also, white wine should be stored and served cold.

- **Riesling**
  In aromatic, delicate, and elegant wine with flavors ranging from a variety of fruits to honey to light minerals.

- **Chardonnay**
  Possibly the most popular varietal, with complex aromas of nuts, butter, toast, apple, peach, and lemon. The California versions have pronounced oak notes.

- **Chenin Blanc**
  This grape is capable of producing some of the finest sweet wines, and it also makes some sparkling wines. The dry versions usually have a greater intensity of honey and fruits such as apples and apricots.

- **Sauvignon Blanc**
  In Bordeaux, this grape is often blended with Semillon and is also known as Fume Blanc and Pouilly-Fume. Known for its grassy, herbal, and citrus flavors. The California versions usually have melon, fig and creamy notes.

- **Chablis**
  True Chablis comes from the Chablis region of France and is made from 100% Chardonnay Grape. In keeping with the French style, the aging process is not done in oak barrels, nor is oak added in any way.

- **Pinot Blanc**
  A part of the pinot grape family that includes Pinot Gris and Pinot Grigio. Pinot Blanc is flexible with food, ranges from very dry to richly sweet wine, and has similar buttery, apple flavors to an un-oaked Chardonnay.

Food Matching

Many believe that certain wines should be enjoyed with certain types of foods. While you don't have to live with the pairings, the traditional mandate is white wines with fish, poultry and pork dishes and red wines with meats - balancing the weight of the food with that of the wine. Here are some suggestions:

- **Chicken** - Chardonnay and Pinot Noir (both good especially with sauces and fried dishes), Sauvignon Blanc (grilled and roasted dishes), and Pinot Blanc.

- **Duck** - a medium bodied, juicy Pinot Noir, Merlot, and Chardonnay

- **Mild Fish** - Riesling, Sauvignon Blanc, Zinfandel, and Chardonnay (usually the less oaked variety). Pinot Noir blends well with pan-fried tuna, and salmon is great with Merlot.

- **Seafood** - Chablis (light shellfish such as oysters and clams), Riesling, Chardonnay (fatty shellfish - lobster, shrimp - with buttery sauces), any light to medium white Pinot wines.
- **Red Meats and Red Sauces** - Red Sauces should be served with the wines with which they are made, and the heavier the sauce, the bolder the wine.
- **Lamb** - Red Zinfandel, Cabernet, Pinot Noir, and Red Burgundy.
- **Beef** - With roast beef - Cabernet and Zinfandel. With stews you could have a Syrah, Pinot Noir or Cabernet
- **Veal** - Red Burgundy, Bordeaux, and Merlot. Pinot Noir is the optimal wine for Osso Buco.

Choosing A Wine

It is best to have an idea of what you wish to eat before selecting a wine, but you can never go wrong with simply choosing what you like. The lighter wines are usually great on their own, and a good choice if you wish to branch out and try something new. At a restaurant, the sommelier is a great resource.

Wine Temperature

White wines and rosés are best served between 45 and 55 degrees. Serve the lighter types and champagnes closer to 45 degrees. Serving temperatures can be achieved by chilling for about 2 hours. If too cold, let it sit out for about 15 minutes. Red wines are best between 55 and 65 degrees, with the lighter closer to 55 degrees. Keep in a cool spot and chill for a short time if preferred on the cooler side.

Tasting Wines

Swish the glass. Look at the color, see if there's sediment. Sniff. Is the aroma good? Sip. Try to get the essence of the wine. The cork is given to let you see if there is discoloration or rot. If it looks nasty, then the bottle may be bad.

Glasses

For white wines you want a tulip shaped glass with long, slender stems, while a red wine should be served in a wider rimmed, shorter stemmed glass.

Leftover Wine

Both red and white unfinished wines can be stored in the refrigerator for 3 to 5 days, or can be used for cooking.

> *" He who has wine and meat will have many friends. ""*

Chinese Proverb

HELPFUL WEB SITES

- www.fosters.com.au/wine
- www.wineenthusiast.com
- www.wine.com
- www.wineanswers.com

Stock Your Bar Like A Barkeep

Everyone has ..."their drink," - the old standby they order at weddings, bars, and after successful parole hearings. To make visitors feel comfortable when they come by, follow our preparatory suggestions for your thirsty friends.

Decide What Your Friends Drink
Are your friends a wine and beer crowd? Or are they mixed-drink crowd? Stock based on what your friends drink, not stuff that will just gather dust.

Alcohol
Here is a quick list of basic bottles your bar should feature: bourbon, scotch, rum, vodka, vermouth, white wine, and red wine.

Beer
You may also want to offer a variety of different types. There are two major types of beers, "lagers" and "ales." Lagers are usually paler, drier, and have less alcohol than ales. Lagers include such types of beer as "pilsners," while ales include "porters" and "stouts."

Ice
Make sure that you have enough ice to keep the beer cold, and for mixed drinks.

Garnishes/Mixers
Olives, lemon, lime, cherries, grenadine, and lime juice.

Mixers
Be ready with juices, tonic water, and various soft drinks.

Equipment
If you have the following items you will be pretty well set: bottle opener, corkscrew, juicer, blender, cocktail shaker, ice bucket, and jigger.

Recipes
While new drinks and shots are created daily, and can be found in bartender books or on the internet, here are a couple of old standbys:

- **Mint Julep**
  1 1/4 oz. bourbon, 1 tbsp. simple syrup, mint leaves, ice. Serve in a highball glass.

- **Amaretto Sour**
  1 1/4 oz. amaretto, 4 oz. sweet and sour mix, crushed ice. Serve in bar glass.

- **Dry Martini**
  1 1/8 oz. gin, 1/8 oz. dry vermouth, garnished with olive. Serve in martini glass.
- **Gin and Ginger**
  1 1 /4 oz. gin, ginger ale.
- **Hurricane**
  3/4 oz. dark rum, 1 /2 oz. light rum, juice from 1/2 lime, 1 tbsp. passion fruit juice. Pour over crushed ice and garnish with a lime.
- **Manhattan**
  1 oz. whisky, 1/4 oz. vermouth, 1 dash bitters. Garnished with cherry and served on the rocks or chilled.

Glasses
There are several types of glasses that your bar should have, including martini glasses, champagne glasses, shot glasses, wine glasses, highball glasses, and beer glasses/steins. Everything seems to taste better when served in a nice glass. You've outgrown those plastic fraternity cups.

Blenders
Depending on your taste preferences, your friends, and time of year you may want to have blended drinks, so you'll need a blender that can handle your ice-crushing needs.

Responsibility
As it is your responsibility to make sure that your guests have the right drinks, it is also your responsibility to help avoid the deadly mix of drinking and driving. Offer cabs, think about designated drivers, or provide a place to crash.

HELPFUL WEB SITES
- www.crateandbarrel.com
- www.webtender.com
- www.epicurious.com/drinking
- www.idrink.com

Kitchen Tips

Well it is time to leave behind the pizza boxes and pop cans. Dinner parties with friends are a great way to stay in contact after college. The kitchen is one of the most used rooms in a home, but it can be intimidating to equip. In reality, the kitchen is not as difficult to outfit as you might think - just start with the basics and you will be at the head of the table in no time.

Utensils

Cooking can be a messy adventure. Having the right utensils makes a difference. In most situations, nylon utensils are better to use because they will not scratch your pots and pans. Here is a list of some good kitchen tools to have:

- Long handled spoon to stir
- Spatula
- Spiral whisk
- Pizza cutter
- Can opener
- Vegetable peeler
- Cork screw
- Scissors
- Manual food chopper
- Set of knives - see below
- Knife sharpener

Knives

It's all about having the right tool for the job. Sharp kitchen knives can make the time in the kitchen not only more enjoyable, but more productive. A good set of knives is worth the investment. The best blades are made of either high-carbon steel or high-carbon stainless steel. While the stainless steel is just that, stainless, the high-carbon steel blades will tarnish over time, but they take a better edge, are easier to maintain, and are more flexible. Some knives to have include:

- 3" paring knife (performs small tasks)
- 4" vegetable knife (also good for fruit)
- 5" utility knife (for jobs too large for the paring knife)
- 6" boning knife (designed to do as it sounds -separate meat from the bone)
- 8" bread knife (slices bread, rolls and boneless meats)
- 8" slicing/carving knife (use to cut thin, uniform slices -its pointed tip helps cut around bones)
- 8" chef's knife (this knife has a wide curved blade designed with enough clearance so you can mince and dice without your knuckles hitting the cutting board)
- 4.5" steak knives (good to slice and trim steaks and other meats)

Bowls And Stuff

- Measuring cups
- Measuring spoons
- Mixing bowls
- Cutting block
- Cheese cutting board with cutter
- Oven mitt
- Food processor

Cookware

- 1 1/2 quart covered saucepan
- 2 quart covered saucepan
- 4 quart casserole with lid
- 10 inch skillet
- Oven pans 9x9 or 9x13
- Muffin pan
- Casserole dish
- Cookie sheet

Appliances

- Rice cooker
- Crock pot
- Bread maker

Other Pieces

Whether you pre-made food to help cut the cooking load before a meal or if you just finished cooking and have leftovers, these are a few of the basic disposables to have on hand:

- Parchment paper
- Aluminum foil
- Plastic wrap
- Plastic bags
- Plastic containers

Some Flavor

You'll likely need to season your dishes, so have the following around your house:

- Salt and Pepper
- Cayenne Pepper
- Red Pepper Flakes
- Basil
- Thyme
- Rosemary
- Garlic Powder
- Garlic Salt
- Lemon Pepper
- Steak Seasoning
- Brown Sugar
- Cilantro
- Cinnamon
- Cumin
- Dill Weed
- Ginger
- Mustard Seed
- Nutmeg
- Oregano
- Paprika
- Tarragon

Recipes

The last ingredient that will complete your kitchen is a recipe book. This can be as formal as some of the well-known cookbooks on the market, or as informal as a small scrapbook to start building your own favorite recipes. Also, many chefs now post their recipes on the internet, so if you see a dish on a tv show, check out the show's website to get the recipe. Finally, ask relatives for their recipes. They'll likely see it as a compliment and would love to help you out.

> *" Part of the secret of a success in life is to eat what you like and let the food fight it out inside. "*
>
> Mark Twain

HELPFUL WEB SITES

- www.foodtv.com
- www.cooking.com
- www.epicurious.com
- www.yankeegrocery.com/spice_mill/yhspgloss.html

Entertaining Formally

Do you love putting on a penguin suit or dressing up? If the answer is "yes," then why not throw your own little soiree. In order to entertain formally, one must plan ahead. As long as you remain organized and think ahead, you'll throw a party people will be talking about for weeks!

Audience
One of the most important things to remember is who the party is for - who will be your audience? Keep the party's theme in mind, if there is one, and tailor invitations, entertainment, even food around it. For themes, think about what your age group is and what people will be wearing (who wants to play board games in a tux?).

Timeline
Set a date for the party. Then, establish target dates for the various steps along the way - invitations, decorations, food, etc. Talk to your caterers, florists, and others to get their timelines.

Location
Look around for a location for the party. Make sure to keep the season in mind when choosing a spot. Don't forget to ask about capacity. Ask about cost. Find out if deposits are required, and if they are refundable. Be sure to ask what hours you have, and if and when you have to do "tear down." How many cars, trucks will you need? Also, it helps if you ask for a floor plan/layout so you can organize your team for the evening/ day of the event.

Food
If you are catering a party, you can begin by coming in with a menu of your own or let the caterer create one for you. Either way, work with a budget. Don't be afraid to remind the caterer of your financial restraints.

Rentals
Be sure to get a quote. It is best to know the number of guests before you start. If your budget allows, rent the linens, tables, table settings (plates, silverware and glasses), and chairs. If you're having the place at a banquet hall or public site like a museum, ask if tables and chairs are included in their price. If you only need to rent linens, sometimes the caterer can organize that.

Entertainment
Figure out what type of party you want to have. If you want a band, D.J., or magician, check with local agencies or even the yellow pages.

Seating

Are you going to have place cards? Will it be a sit-down meal, or will there just be hors d'ouvres? If you're having an elderly crowd, think about keeping them away from the speakers blasting out heavy metal music.

Invitations

Create an RSVP deadline date, then set a date to mail the invitations. The RSVP date, which is a date that will be printed on the invitation, forces you to send the invitations on time. Pick out invitations. If you are making your own invitations or having them printed, start creating the design, and getting printing quotes.

Actual Event

In order to be able to enjoy the evening, you just have to be flexible and expect things to change from your original plan.

HELPFUL WEB SITES

- www.directcatering.com
- www.alltimefavorites.com
- www.foodnetwork.com/food/entertaining
- http://entertaining.about.com

Entertaining Informally

Are your friends itching to get together? Do you owe them a good time? Well then, it's time for a party. Check out the following list to help you get your informal party off the ground, and to keep your pad safe.

Date
When do you want to have your little get together? Pick a date that will give you time to prep and clean up.

Purpose
Needs will vary, depending on the reason for your party. Pony rides for your friends will dictate a ton of tarps for your apartment. If you are just having a get together in your apartment, you'll want to clear out room and give your neighbors a heads up (even consider inviting them over, they'll be less likely to call the cops). If you want to throw a barbecue, or anything outside, have a plan in case of rain.

Invites
Technology is so great that you don't have to spend time and money sending real invitations. Use your email address book and online invite services to send out invitations, reminders, and to keep track of your RSVPs. If you do want to send real invitations, think about prepackaged cards and envelopes that fit your theme, or even make your own online using a photo website.

Food
Make sure that you have enough food for your friends, and your friends' friends. Think about going to a warehouse store to get "industrial sized" mayonnaise and packs of 64 hot dog buns. You can always freeze your extra food, and eat it for the next two weeks. If you're serving something a little more sophisticated than burgers and hot dogs, consider short cuts, such as pre-made salads and foods that you can prepare ahead of time.

Drinks
The drinks depend on the crowd, but remember you can control it. If you want to have alcohol, but don't want to spend a lot, get a keg, or have "cheap beer night" or something that fits your budget. Also, remember to have non-alcoholic drinks. Finally, don't forget the ice.

Paper Goods

To make clean-up easy, consider getting paper plates, plastic cups, and plastic forks. If you entertain a lot, stock up so you're always ready for a party. Grab a permanent marker so friends can mark their cups.

Entertainment

Plan ahead. Check out the details on the boxing match you want to buy on pay-per view, make a mixed CD, or make a playlist on your MP3 player, and get the games/cards together, etc. Being prepared will make everything less hectic.

HELPFUL WEB SITES

- www.askmen.com/fashion/how_to/18b_how_to.html
- www.evite.com
- www.foodnetwork.com/food/entertaining
- www.diynetwork.com/diy/le_theme_parties/0,2040,DIY_14029,00.html

Party Ideas

Want to make some new friends or catch up with some people that you haven't seen in a while? Then throw a killer party. No, it doesn't have to be a murder mystery party, but that's not a bad idea. Below are some party tips and ideas, so go get some streamers, goofy hats, and noisemakers.

Costume Party
Halloween is an obvious time for a costume party, but isn't it more fun to have your friends walk around in public dressed as cavemen in the middle of July?

Murder Mystery Parties
These are parties where everyone plays a role in a murder mystery. You can pick up murder mystery games at your local bookstore.

Game Nights
This is a throwback to the days where you would play games all night with your friends. Now, hipper games are being made daily. Games such as Cranium and Trivia Pursuit are great for groups of friends. You could also go old school and play things like Candyland, Clue, Twister, charades, Monopoly, Trivial Pursuit or bingo and relive your childhood.

Cards/Casino
Get a bunch of chips and friends together and play cards. You could even invest in a craps table or a roulette wheel and have your own casino.

Food Themed Parties
Parties are a great excuse to make a certain kind of food the centerpiece of the fiesta. Buffalo wings, 6 foot long subs, fondue, sushi are all cool choices.

Sports Night
Big sports fan? If you are, why not invite some friends over to watch the game. You can wear jerseys and cheer like you've never cheered before.

Trivia Night
Consider buying a trivia game or make your own trivia questions with an almanac, the internet, and a bunch of index cards.

Karaoke
The '80s are back. Rent a karaoke machine and invite your pals over for a night of singin' fun. Come on, how long has it been since you've sung "Living on a Prayer" or "I Will Survive"?

Movie Night/TV Night

You can have everyone over for a movie-themed night - such as cheesy '80s movies, or thrillers. If you're not into movies, you can watch Seinfeld reruns or Saved by the Bell. If you do this, have everyone come over dressed as their favorite character from the show.

Holiday Parties

You can coordinate activities with drinks and food. For example, on Halloween, you can serve pumpkin pie, and the activity could be carving pumpkins or dunking for apples.

Music Appreciation Night

You can have a party where you only play one band, or music from a particular decade. Who wouldn't love a night filled with 80's Rock?

Pot Luck/Bake Off

Have your friends pitch in by bringing their best recipes. You could even have a bake off contest. See who can make the best brownies or tuna casserole. The winner could get a crown & and sash.

Craft Night

Tie-Dye, puzzles, jewelry, knit....invite over your pals for a night 'o crafts.

Foam Party

If you're into messiness, convert your apartment into a foam room.

Slumber Party

For the guys out there, you can watch movies, eat popcorn, play truth or dare, and paint each other's nails.

HELPFUL WEB SITES

- www.askmen.com/fashion/how_to/18b_how_to.html
- www.diynet.com/diy/lv_entertaining/0,2040,DIY_14108,00.html
- www.diynetwork.com/diy/le_party_planning/0,2040,DIY_14027,00.html

Poker

If the last time you played cards your game was go-fish and your cards had cartoon bears on them, then maybe you want to think about advancing a bit and start playing a little poker.

What Is It?
While the term "poker" does not refer to a certain game, there are some that are more popular than others.

Some Terms To Know
- "Ante" is an initial contribution by all players to fund the pot.
- "Blind" is similar to an ante, being a forced bet by one or more players. Blinds are used in hold'em games.
- "Burn" is the term used when a card from the community deck is discarded to ensure against cheating.
- "Check" is to not bet, but stay in the game, having the option to bet or fold later.
- "No Limit" is a game of poker where one may bet any amount.
- "Flop" are the initial 3 community cards that are placed face up.
- "Turn" is the fourth community card placed face up.
- "River" is the fifth, and final community card.

Some Games

Texas Hold'Em
Every player is dealt two cards face down. There is a round of betting followed by the "flop," which is the turning over of three cards out of the deck (a burn is optional). Another round of betting is completed, followed by the "turn" and more betting. Next comes the "river" and the final betting. Players will use their two cards and the five community to make the best poker hand.

Omaha
Every player is dealt four cards face down. There is a round of betting followed by the "flop," which is the turning over of three cards out of the deck (a burn is optional). Another round of betting is completed, followed by the "turn," more betting, and the "river." The difference between Omaha and Texas Hold'Em is that you can only use two cards from your hand out of the four. So if you have four Aces in your hand, sorry, you can only use two.

Poker Hands From Lowest To Highest

- High Cards - If there are no pairs, no straight, and no flush, then the game is usually won by the player with the highest card. Tiebreakers are won by the next highest cards in the hand.

- Pair

- Two Pair

- Three of a Kind

- Straight - 5 cards in sequence, but not of the same suit

- Flush - 5 cards of the same suit (diamonds, clubs, hearts, spades), but not in sequence

- Full House - Three of a kind and a pair

- Four of Kind

- Straight Flush - 5 cards that are in sequence and of the same suit (a royal straight flush is a 10, J, Q, K, A of the same suit)

Equipment

For a night of poker you'll likely need at least two decks of cards, so that your evening is not spent shuffling cards, poker chips (casino type chips are more expensive and made of clay), and a big table (you can even get felt tops to put on your table).

HELPFUL WEB SITES

- www.thepokerforum.com/pokerterms.htm
- www.poker-press.com/home/home_default.asp
- www.pagat.com/vying/poker.html
- www.partypoker.net
- www.pokerchips.com

HITTING
THE ROAD

section
06

133

How To Buy A Car

Buying a car can be a really big hassle and a very stressful experience, or it can be really pleasant. How do you make sure you're getting the best deal? Keep an open mind, and remember that knowledge is power. Have a little fun, too.

Research

If you are buying a new car, use the internet. It's one of the best resources available for finding the invoice price of a vehicle (what the dealer pays for it) and the MSRP (sticker). Just make sure if you are looking for a specific vehicle, that the invoice includes any accessories/options you're looking for. Learn about "day's supply" - manufacturers try to stock inventories with certain numbers of cars. If inventory is out of balance - an oversupply - dealers may be willing to slash their profit.

Avoid Hot Vehicles

No, don't go for a vehicle no one wants. You want to make sure your car is safe and reliable. However, if you're dying to have a car that's in demand, don't expect a discount. If a car is hard to come by, you can bet a salesperson will sell what's available to the highest bidder.

Mechanics Are Your Friends

If you're trading in your current vehicle, have your mechanic look it over, and ask him to give you a rough appraisal, before going to a dealership. Also, if you're buying a used car, ask if you can take it to your mechanic. The dealership will only say no if it's a shady place.

Background Check

For a used vehicle, always have the dealership run a history check to make sure the car wasn't involved in any accidents. Also, look to see if the car was a rental. Rentals have a reputation for being more beat-up than the average used vehicle.

Don't Expect A Bargain

Salespeople are not crooks, but they are trying to make a living. Don't expect them to give you a deal because you're ready to buy. Ask for the discount. Cars are marked up about 8-10%, but a 3-4% markup is a decent profit for the dealership, and a good deal for you.

Be Aware Of Dealer-Installed Items

Pinstripes are nice, as are door-edge guards. But these things do not come free. Any added package is marked way up for extra profit. If the options are on the vehicle already, don't expect to get them free. However, you can expect to get them at cost.

Insurance

That sporty car may look pretty cool, but you can bet the insurance will be a lot higher than on a more conservative vehicle.

Educational Discounts

Check with your dealer to see if graduate discounts exist, as you may be able to save some money.

Lemon Laws

Check out your state's lemon laws if you have problems with your new car.

HELPFUL WEB SITES

- www.kbb.com
- www.edmunds.com
- www.autobytel.com
- www.carbuyingtips.com
- www.carfax.com
- http://bbb.com/alerts/article.asp?ID=433
- http://bbb.com/alerts/article.asp?ID=432

Renting A Car

If you are sick of driving around in your old sedan and want to look flashy on your trip to _____ (insert sunny city), treat yourself to a brand new convertible. No, we're not talking about using your hotwiring skills, we're talking about renting a car. Here are some topics you need to consider.

Are You Old Enough?
Many rental companies require drivers to be a minimum of 18 years old, while others require drivers to be 25. Some companies may charge extra for drivers under 25, so be aware. If, by chance, you do not meet the company age requirement, ask if membership in certain organizations will allow you to rent at a younger age.

What Size Do You Want/Need?
What is the purpose of your trip? Will you be zipping up and down the coast or offroading, or will you be transporting family members around all weekend?

Booking A Car
There are several avenues. You can call a travel agent who may know of specials and local companies. Other options include booking a package trip that includes a car, or checking out internet specials.

Confirmation Code
Make sure that you have a copy of your confirmation code when you go to pick up your car. It will make it faster and easier.

Classification Systems
Rental companies like making cars sound much better than they are, like designating a car that only two normal-sized people could fit into as a "luxury" car. So, make sure that you clarify what car models are in each class. You may even be able to see pictures of the classifications on the company's web site.

Insurance
Check with your insurance carrier at home prior to renting any vehicle, as they may cover any accidents in a rental car. Also, if you are on a business trip and renting a car, talk with your employer about its insurance coverage.

Getting A Deal
Ask your rental company if there are specials on certain classes of cars (mid-size, luxury, convertible). There may be deals for weekend/weekday rentals. Also, if you belong to any organizations (AAA, ABA, honors associations, fraternity, sorority, etc.) ask to see if the rental company has special offers. Also, ask if there are any add-ons, which would change your rate.

Gas

Fully understand the gas situation on your receiving and returning of the car. If you have to return the car with a full tank, make sure that you do so, or the rental company may charge an exorbitant rate for their gas. Also, remember what time you have to return the car (i.e. whether you have an early morning flight) so that you plan refueling properly.

Extra Fees

Check out other fees, such as taxes, airport charges, additional drivers fees, etc. that you may have to pay. Also, if you want to drop your car off at a different location from that which you took the car from, there may be an additional charge.

Traveling Internationally

Do research on the traffic laws of the foreign country, what your insurance coverage will be, and if an international driver's license is necessary prior to leaving the U.S.

Get Directions/Maps

Ask for directions and local maps (they're usually free).

Bring Your Cell Phone

A cell phone can come in handy when driving in a new city. Make sure you keep the phone number of your rental agency nearby along with the phone number of your destination.

Rental Company Programs

If you travel a lot, consider joining rental company programs to get specials, benefits, and incentives.

Frequent Flyer

Ask your company if they give airline frequent flyer mileage for your rental.

HELPFUL WEB SITES

- www.ftc.gov/bcp/conline/pubs/autos/carrent.htm
- www.travelsense.org/tips/car.asp
- www.http://bbb.com/alerts/article.asp?ID=96
- www.hertz.com
- www.enterprise.com

Detailing Your Car

Got a hot date you want to impress? Want to show off your ride to the guys down at the corner, or across the street, or perhaps down the block - well wherever the guys are, here are some detailing tips.

The Tools
Go to your local retailer and arm yourself with the products you'll need. Ask for their advice and recommendations on special products. You should stick with name brands and see if there are kits that contain many of the products you'll need. Below is a quick list of some tools:

- Hose
- Bucket
- Interior Cleaner/Conditioner
- Compressed Air Can (computer keyboard cleaner) for all the nooks and crannies of your car
- Feather Duster
- Glass Cleaner
- Sheepskin Wash Mittens
- Car Wash Soap
- Carpet Cleaner
- Bug and Tar Remover
- Specialty Brush for Wheels
- Terry Cloth Towel or Chamois
- Polish or Wax
- Wheel Cleaner
- Tire Cleaner
- Plastic Polish
- Toothbrush (for leftover wax residue)
- General Purpose Cleaner
- Sponges
- Convertible Top Cleaner (if applicable)
- Cotton Swabs
- Vacuum
- Paper Towels

Directions

Make sure you read all directions on the products and consult your owner's manual.

The Order

A logical order to detailing is important. Do the interior first, as the dirt and particles you dust out will get stuck on your exterior. Then move onto the outside of the car. Here is a sample order:

- Interior
- Vacuum
- Wipe clean all surfaces
- Dashboard and all vents - use the swabs and compressed air
- Windows
- Trunk
- Wash
- Rinse with water
- Wash with water and the right soap using the mittens
- Use specialty cleaners on stubborn spots
- Wash wheels and tires last
- Rinse once more
- Dry
- Polish and Wax
- Don't forget the crannies
- Use brush to clean out the wheels
- Polish your plastic on the outside of your car
- Final Touches
- Check out emblems and moldings to clean off wax residue
- Outside glass

HELPFUL WEB SITES

- www.carcrazy.net/tips.htm
- www.web-cars.com/detail
- www.http://autorepair.about.com/od/carcare

Public Transportation Tips

There's enough stress in life without having to worry about finding a parking spot or making sure you paid the meter, so relax and take public transportation. Besides a hassle free commute, you're bound to meet some very "interesting" characters. Below you'll find info and tips for some major U.S. cities.

New York

- **Subway**
  It mostly takes you uptown and downtown. Each line, represented by a different color, has a local and express track. At some stops you can transfer from local to express, while at other stops you can transfer from one line to another.

- **Buses**
  Probably the best way to get across town and through the park and can be very efficient during the middle of the day when there is no rush hour. Buses don't make change, so you'll need exact fare or a pass. Unlimited passes are available, so consider one if you'll use the bus a lot.

- **Taxis**
  This is the most infamous method of transportation in NYC, as you'll not only get somewhere, but also likely have a white-knuckle experience. If you can find your seat belt, you should definitely use it. One thing to remember is that if you know the fastest route to where you're going be sure to speak up.

Washington, D.C.

- **Metro Trains:**
  Trains are labeled by colors and by direction. The orange line can take you to the Smithsonian, the National Gallery of Art, the National Archives, and many other great spots. The blue line takes you to Arlington Cemetery, National (Reagan) Airport, and the Pentagon. The red line can take you to Chinatown and Union Station, which houses the Amtrak trains.

- **Metra Bus:**
  Stops are easy to identify, as they have red, white, and blue signs or flags. Make sure to have a pass or exact change when you board the bus. Make sure to check for transfers when changing buses or from trains to buses.

Chicago

- **The Subway**
  Chicago is famous for its partially elevated rail system, which has led to its name "The El." You can tell where you're going by looking at the platform signs or the signs on the trains themselves. There are lines, differentiated by color. Look into buying passes and transit cards.

- **Bus System**
  The Chicago Transit Authority offers bus service throughout the city. You can save money by purchasing a pass, so make sure to check out the savings and your intended amount of use of the system.

San Francisco

- **The Muni**
  The San Francisco Municipal Railway provides buses and trains throughout the city. You can take it downtown or out to the beach. The "F" line is the historic streetcar line that includes renovated streetcars from the U.S. and Europe. Make sure that you have coins for the subway turnstiles. Look into monthly passes to save money and hassle.

- **The BART**
  Bay Area Rapid Transit is the best way to come into the city from the 'burbs. BART fares are calculated based on destination. Remember, BART stops running at midnight, so make sure to catch your train or find a place to crash.

- **The Cable Car**
  San Francisco is famous for the Cable Car. Its main purpose was to battle the steep hills, and it still continues to do so. You can use a Muni-Pass to save some bucks.

HELPFUL WEB SITES

- www.mta.nyc.ny.us
- www.wmata.com
- www.transitchicago.com
- www.chicago-l.org
- www.bart.gov
- www.transitinfo.org
- www.sfmuni.com

Buying Auto Insurance

Did you just get some flames painted on the side of your car and can't wait to take it for a spin? Well, make sure you have auto insurance, a necessary evil, but one that will allow you to drive that flame - mobile legally. You don't have to overpay, however, and you need to learn a little to help understand this complicated topic.

Choosing A Car Insurance Carrier

Look for an agent you like and feel comfortable with. Ask friends and family for recommendations, and find out how these agents have handled claims in the past. You also will want a company that is financially strong. Finally, you want a good price, so make sure to check around.

Pricing

When looking for policies make sure to get several quotes. Various websites will allow you to comparison shop online. You can ask for higher deductibles as a way to keep your payments down. Some factors that will be used to determine your price will be:

- Your car
- Your driving experience, including years driving and accident history
- Where you drive
- Amount of coverage you want
- Remember to check your driving record to make sure there are no mistakes that may influence your policy's price.

Coverage

Don't leave yourself exposed, get as much insurance as you can afford, and make sure you have coverage for the various exposures out there. Make sure you read each policy carefully to understand the extent of your coverage and when each is invoked. Common kinds of coverage include:

- **Collision**
  This coverage pays for damage to your auto from a collision.

- **Bodily Injury/Liability**
  Protection from claims made against you for causing bodily injury in a crash. This policy will also cover defense costs.

- **Comprehensive**
  This covers damage to your car from anything other than an accident, such as vandalism or theft.

- **Medical**
  This will cover injuries for people in your car.

Insurance Discounts

There are many ways to reduce the costs of your policy. Make sure you talk with your agent about safety features your car offers and yourself as a driver. Some types of discounts include:

- Air bags
- Car alarms
- Anti-lock brakes
- Your make and model of car
- Your age
- Your marital status
- Safe Driver

HELPFUL WEB SITES

- www.allstate.com/Products/Auto/PageRender.asp?Page=main.htm
- www.esurance.com
- www.bbb.org/alerts/article.asp?ID=431
- www.bbb.org/alerts/article.asp?ID=86
- http://statefarm.com/insuranc/auto/auto.htm

How To Pack For A Trip

So, you've got a big trip ahead of you. You're going to visit your Aunt Sadie in beautiful Bismarck, North Dakota. Ahh, hours of waiting for flights and the hope of finding basic cable at your aunt's house. Check out the following packing tips to have the most enjoyable trip, and to assure you have the proper dinner dress for the one restaurant that stays open past 5:30.

Plan Your Days
Think about what you'll be doing each day and what attire will be necessary. Will you be swimming? Frequenting restaurants that require jackets? Will you be taking leisurely walks? Pack clothing that corresponds to your schedule.

Pack Clothes That Go Together
Pick out outfits before packing. Think about outfits that can be interchanged. Can you wear different shirts with the same pants? Can you use a sports coat with different shirts? Can you match different tops with the same skirt? You may also want to pack clothes that go together in order, so you're not rooting through all your clothes to find matching pieces.

Check Out The Weather
Before you head to Seattle without a raincoat or go to Palm Springs during the summer with only pants and sweatshirts, you'll want to know the forecast. Consider packing clothes that layer together well if the weather varies.

Shoes
Make sure you bring the right shoes for the right occasion. You want shoes that are comfortable and versatile. You don't want to be stuck wearing tennis shoes with a gray suit. Also, remember to keep clothes away from any smelly shoes, so think about clothing placement and bringing plastic bags for shoes.

Jewelry
Forecast what you'll be wearing. Will you be attending formal events on your trip that require cuff links or a nice necklace, or will you be hanging out with friends on the beach? Think about where you will put the jewelry too; if it's expensive you probably don't want to put it in your packed luggage, but should wear it. Depending on where you'll be traveling, you may not want to call attention to your jewelry.

Folding

There are different styles of folding, but it's good to fold your clothes in a way that will allow the most space in your luggage. You may try rolling t-shirts or packing ties, belts and socks inside your shoes.

Toiletries

Make sure you remember a toothbrush, toothpaste, razor, shaving cream, brush/comb, deodorant, contacts and solution, glasses, aspirin, and any other toiletries you use daily. Pack them in a carry-on bag so you don't get stuck without your glasses or a toothbrush when you land in San Francisco and your luggage lands in Cleveland. You may also want to pack medications for allergies or diarrhea. Bring some antacids. Think about going prepared with antibiotics and getting the proper shots if traveling abroad. Finally, it's a smart move to pack liquids, creams, and lotions in a plastic bag so you won't smell like a piña colada for the whole trip.

Carry On Luggage

These days many travelers avoid checking luggage, which can save waiting time. If you do want to carry on your luggage, confirm that you have the right size with the airline beforehand.

Entertainment

Think about how much time you'll be sitting around. Be prepared with books, magazines, playing cards, or DVD's for your laptop. MP3 players are great because you can have a ton of music in such a small space. Also, digital cameras will alleviate the worry of X-Ray machines ruining your film.

Stay In Touch

Remember your cell phone charger and phone cards.

HELPFUL WEB SITES

- www.travelsense.org/tips/packing.asp
- www.weather.com
- www.tsa.gov/public/interapp/editorial/editorial_1052.xml

Getting Deals On Hotels

Everyone wants a deal. So why settle for anything else. It's becoming rare to see hotel guests pay rack rate, with competition growing stronger among hotels. Discounts run rampant, but you have to know where to look.

Weekday vs. Weekend

Depending on a hotel's demand, room rates may be different on certain days. Hotels do this to attract more business (e.g. weekend packages or weekday getaways). Always ask if the nightly rate will be the same throughout the entire stay.

Best Rate

Almost every hotel reserves a "best rate" for price-sensitive customers. Ask if that is their best rate after getting a quote.

Internet Specials

It is often cheaper for a hotel to sell rooms directly through their own website, instead of paying a 3rd party (Expedia, Orbitz, etc.). While these third-party companies sometimes have the lowest rates, try the hotel's website first. Packages, as well as internet rates, frequently show up. You might be surprised!

3rd Party Affiliates

If a hotel does not have a website, try the major discount travel websites. Hotels with lots of empty rooms discount heavily. Most sites offer a wide range of hotels, from economy to upscale. But be careful - some discount sites have cancellation/change restrictions. Know what you are getting into before booking.

Major Affiliates / Organizations

Many hotels have relationships with groups and organizations that provide discounts. AAA and AARP are among the most popular. Ask a hotel if it honors any membership discount.

Friendliness Has Its Advantages

Just like in any service industry, front-line employees have a lot more power than you might expect. Being friendly while making a reservation encourages the reservationists to work harder for you - either finding you a deal or upgrading your reservation. This is true at check-in as well. Always wear a smile and be friendly. If you are rude, you may just end up in a small room.

Rewards Programs

If you travel a lot, you may consider joining a hotel's rewards program. Almost every large hotel chain offers some type of a program and can be beneficial at each visit, as well as providing discounts to other services, such as car rentals and airlines.

> *Though we travel the world over to find the beautiful, we must carry it with us or we find it not.*
>
> Ralph Waldo Emerson

HELPFUL WEB SITES

- www.orbitz.com
- www.expedia.com
- www.hotels.com
- www.cheaptickets.com
- www.priceline.com
- www.bbb.org/alerts/article.asp?ID=444

Picking A Hotel

Hotel rooms aren't your standard roadside flophouses anymore, but places with CD alarm clocks, video game consoles, and all the towels you want. With so many hotels to choose from, which one is best for you? Here are some things to think about when looking for a room.

Style
Today's hotels differentiate themselves based on unique atmospheres — ranging from ultra-modern to boutique-cozy. What's your style? Do you like having a hip hotel bar where all the rock stars hang out, or do you want a quaint historic room?

Usage
Every hotel targets different groups of customers. Marriott features "Rooms that Work" for business travelers, while Westin features the "Heavenly Bed" for relaxation. What are your needs? Do you need to plug your laptop into a high-speed network? Do you need a suite large enough to conduct business or have a bunch of friends over to crash in?

Amenities
A home away from home — this is every hotel's goal. From fitness facilities to goldfish in your room, there is a hotel that will provide amenities to make you feel welcome. Check out the availability and cost of parking. Think about if you're going to need internet access in your room, and whether the hotel offers any special offers or is a part of a national wireless plan.

Location, Location, Location
If you are visiting a new city, choose a hotel in an area central to your plans. If you are going to be without a vehicle, find a hotel that is near public transportation or has taxi service. Also, see if the hotel offers shuttle service.

Ask Around
Sometimes the best hotels are the ones that are not in the mainstream. Ask your friends and family for suggestions. You might also get some advice on where not to stay!

Points
Many hotel chains are members of frequent flyer programs or offer their own reward programs. If you have a favorite program, see if participating hotels would be a good place to stay.

Star Ratings

Finally, be leery of star ratings. Many hotels claim to be 4-5 star hotels, but whose stars? What defines their stars? Mobil and AAA are the leaders in rating hotels. Take other ratings that are not part of a rating organization with a grain of salt.

" The great advantage of a hotel is that it's a refuge from home life. "

George Bernard Shaw

HELPFUL WEB SITES

- www.mobiltravelguide.com/index.jsp?menu=rating_criteria
- www.morganshotelgroup.com
- www.kimptonhotels.com
- www.aaa.com
- www.historichotels.org
- www.1bbweb.com

Travel Tips For Flying

It's more than likely you've been hosed on a plane ticket purchase. Since you couldn't stay over 4 weeks and travel on alternating Tuesday afternoons, you had to pay the monopolistic piper. Here are some quick hints to help you get a good deal and not get hosed again.

Plan

Know when you want/need to travel, A.S.A.P. The sooner you book, the better your deal will likely be. Think about staying over a Saturday in order to get the best fare. Remember to book well in advance when taking a vacation over the holidays - everyone else is planning on a trip then too.

Arrival/Departure Times

If possible, try various departure and arrival times. Fares may vary depending on capacity. Also, book flights early in the day because flight delays snowball. So if you are traveling at the end of a day filled with delays, you will not only be late, but may even have your flight cancelled.

Good Travel Days

Avoid Sunday returns. That is when volume is the highest. Rates for Tuesdays and Wednesdays are usually lower - they are lower volume travel days.

Email/Internet

Many airlines offer weekly specials announced in emails. If there is a particular airline that you usually fly, go to its website and sign up for any email specials. While on the website, see if they have any special-discount pages for short notice, weekend trips, or packages. Even if you don't use these now, remember them for the future.

Nearby Cities

If you live in a hub city you probably have trouble getting competitive prices. Check out smaller cities within driving distance for better fares. Many low-cost airlines fly into smaller airports, so they'll keep the big carriers honest with lower fares. Even if you don't want to fly the smaller airline, it is more than likely that the major airlines will match prices. You may consider trying to connect through an airport closer to your home so that you can skip your last leg and get home quicker.

Packages

You may be able to get a good buy on combining your airfare, accommodations, and car rentals. Look into working with a wholesale tour operator who negotiates in bulk and can sell to consumers at discounted retail prices.

Frequent Flyer Programs

Frequent flyer programs present a great way to get free tickets or upgrades. Make sure that you get mileage for every trip you take. Even if you forget to get your mileage at the time of purchase, many airlines will allow you to add the mileage to your account later. Also, watch program mailings for specials, such as double mileage for certain months, or for credit cards that allow you to earn miles.

2 for the Price of 1

You can try to get bumped if you are in no big rush to get to your destination. Many airlines will give you a voucher for another flight if you give up your seat and take a later flight. Check with the gate attendant for the policy and whether you can volunteer to give up your seat.

Travel Agents

Good travel agents can be invaluable as they can customize a wholesale package to fit your personality and budget. Also, some of the best tour operators only sell through travel agents. Finally, remember that most travel agents cost you nothing, so make friends with a travel agent.

HELPFUL WEB SITES

- www.princevacations.com
- www.travelocity.com
- www.expedia.com
- www.cheaptickets.com
- www.priceline.com
- www.iflyswa.com
- www.airtran.com
- www.jetblue.com

Road Trip Ideas

So you've got some free time, a set of wheels, a couple of friends, and CD's that you've never listened to all the way through - sounds like it's time for a road trip. The only issues are what to do and where to go. Think about the ideas below.

Baseball Trips

In early spring, you may want to hit up spring training in Florida or Arizona. The games are relaxed, the hot dogs are under $5.00, and you can act like a kid and get autographs. If it's April through October, you can find Major League and Minor League baseball being played throughout the U.S.

Music Trips

Do you have a couple of bands you love but are never in your city? Are there some bands that you've heard are awesome live but you've never seen? If so, then think about hitting the road and sampling these treats. Most bands have websites with touring information. Also, many cities have weekend-long music festivals in the spring and summer.

Elvis Sighting

Why not check out one of the most famous houses in the U.S., Graceland in Memphis, TN. You can get some wicked barbecue and party on Beale Street while you're there.

Festivals

Communities across America put on festivals, from Oktoberfest to Garlic Festivals. Use the internet to find festivals that are within your driving range.

Mardi Gras

If you're anywhere within a 12-hour drive of New Orleans, it is definitely worth hitting this 24-hour-a-day party.

National Parks/Landmarks

National parks are a must for people who love the outdoors. History buffs should consider visiting such places as the White House, the St. Louis Arch, or the Golden Spike in Utah.

Visit Old Friends

Haven't seen some of your friends in a while? Plan a reunion. Pick a city that's central to everyone, and meet up for a weekend.

Love Snow
Snow buds and bunnies need to check out some skiing. There are slopes all over the U.S., so you're not too far away.

Hit The Links
Find a couple of public golf courses and set up a tee time. It's both relaxing and fun, and will allow you and your friends to try and break 120.

College Football
Haven't seen your favorite _____'s (insert mascot name) in a while? Then check out their away schedule, and use the game as an excuse to visit someplace new.

Las Vegas/ Atlantic City
If you're on either coast, think about hitting the blackjack table and a couple of buffets.

Tournament Time
Depending on the time of year, check out college tournaments throughout the country.

HELPFUL WEB SITES
- www.indiefilms.com/bag/filmfest.htm
- www.oktoberfest-zinzinnati.com
- www.tulsaoktoberfest.org
- www.fieldofdreamsmoviesite.com
- www.minorleaguebaseball.com
- www.cactus-league.com
- www.elvis.com
- www.mardigras.com
- www.austinfilmfestival.com
- www.roadtripnation.com
- www.nojazzfest.com
- www.ncaa.org
- www.chuckwagondiner.com/foodfestivals_cookoffs.html

Road Trip Tips

Go Thelma and Louise on a budget — kick off your shoes, blast the music and check out beauty in your own backyard. Now that you have some free time between school and the real world, you should consider heading into the great wide open.

Choosing Your Ride
Although traveling across country in a Hummer could be a great experience, your budget will be shot by the hefty gas prices. If possible, try to use a car that is fuel efficient. If you are lucky at all, check out college bulletin boards for people who want you to drive their car across country. Also, think about vehicle amenities such as CD players, satellite radio, heated seats, etc.

Tuned In
Before you take off, be sure to take the car into an oil and lube place to check your tire pressure (remember the spare), fluid levels, windshield wipers, etc. If you take care of your car, it will be reciprocated. Also make sure that you paid your car insurance payments to avoid overnights in jail.

Getting Lost
Remember there is no such thing because your greatest stories will happen when you take a side trip, "...like the time we got rerouted through Texas and passed a sign that read 'Danger, don't pick up hitch hikers. County Jail 2 miles up.'" If you want to avoid such nights in jail, get directions before heading out.

Your Best Friend
Invest in a good atlas (preferably one that has details of every state). This is sufficient to get you anywhere you want to go. Atlases often come with a map that includes time distances in the back, so that you can estimate your arrival times.

Strapped For Funds?
AAA is your best bet. Don't leave home without a visit (assuming you're a member). Not only do members get discounts on tickets, tourist attractions, hotels etc. but they also hook you up with free books that highlight great lodging, eateries and activities in each major (and many minor) city.

Preventing Road Rage And Frequent Stops
Stock up on fruits, beef jerky, peanuts, bread, peanut butter and jelly, dried fruit etc. This will allow you to cruise to your destination without having to stop frequently. Just remember that you will be in tight quarters when you choose your food, so leave the canned chili at home.

"My Bags Are Packed And ...."

Remember to pack one bag with the essentials that is easily accessible. You will often be taking this bag in and out of the car.

Picture Perfect

Always have your camera ready and accessible in the front seat. You never know what kind of photo opportunity you will have. Also, you are bound to see some beautiful sunrises/sunsets...snap it up!

Cruisin' To The Beat

With so many hours in the car, even your favorite CD's can become trite. Do yourself the favor and make some good tunes. You should definitely have the "emergency mix" when you need a little perking up on the long drive. Consider MP3 players with car adapters, as you can bring your entire collection in your palm. If you're not into music, consider getting books on tape.

Speeding

The "I was going with the speed of traffic" doesn't have the same effect as it used to... remember not to speed in small towns.

Ahhh, The Friends You'll Meet

Truckers can be your greatest friends. They know the rules of the road (pass on your left and move to your right quickly if you are going slower) and often have ways of knowing police officers are lurking ahead. Stick with them and you will be in good company.

Bright Idea

Remember as a courtesy to other drives, turn your bright lights off when passing a car.

Portable Lodging

To keep the expenses down, bring along a tent for those necessary hours of zzzzzzz's without the costly price of motels.

Call Your Peeps

The best way to see some cities is with the locals...so remember your friends and family and CALL THEM!

Document The Trip

Think about bringing along a video camera and digital camera to remember a great trip and even publish a blog from the road.

Inform The Proper Authorities

A good tip is to pass on an agenda to family and friends, so they can find you if need be.

HELPFUL WEB SITES

- www.aaa.com
- www.mapquest.com
- www.roadtripusa.com
- www.roadtripamerica.com

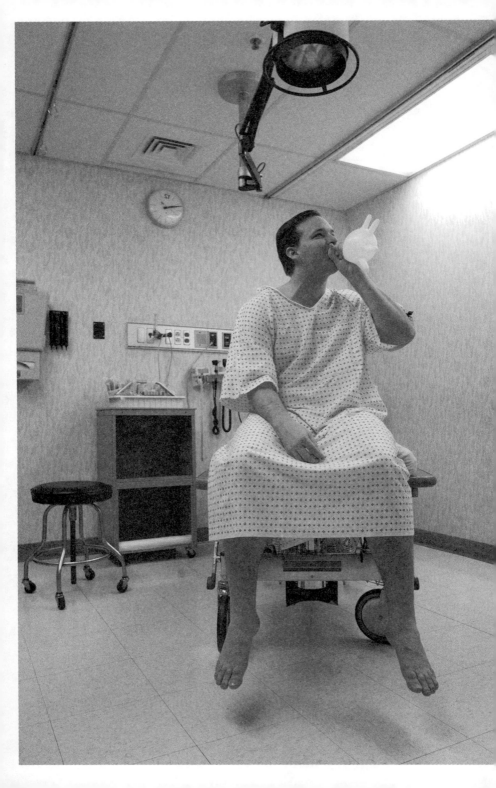

LETTING THE PROFESSIONALS
HANDLE IT

dental tips

eye care tips

section
07

Dental Tips

If you don't mind eating your meals through a straw and never want to eat a jawbreaker again, then please disregard the following. If, though, you want to have a healthy and a beautiful smile well into the future, then keep on reading.

Daily Dental Care
Good dental care consists of brushing your teeth twice a day. Be careful to brush with a light circular motion with a soft bristle brush. Doing otherwise can actually cause your gums to recede. Also, flossing is a must. It is difficult to get into the routine of flossing, but it really is the only way to eliminate the plaque between your teeth. Make sure to rub the floss on both sides of the tooth instead of just popping it in and out. Finally, consider rinsing with an anti-bacterial mouth wash daily.

Picking A Dentist
The best way to choose a dentist is to ask around. A good dentist stays busy because of his or her referrals.

Dental Insurance
Many new graduates begin work with no dental insurance, and it's not needed by everyone. Daily home care and a visit to the dentist every 6 months for a cleaning and check-up are inexpensive ways to provide for a healthy mouth and reduce the risk of living without dental insurance. If, though, you do have dental insurance, most insurance policies allow for $1000 of dental coverage per year. The main disadvantage is that this almost never covers the latest and greatest procedures, such as dental implants, bleaching, and veneers.

Whitening Or Bleaching
To keep it simple, there are three types. The first is over the counter whiteners, which do lighten the shade of your teeth to a degree. However, save your money when it comes to bleaching toothpastes and gums because they really don't work. The second type is at-home prescription bleaching kits. These are gels that are placed into a custom fabricated night guard every night before you go to bed. In about two weeks, you will have noticeably whiter teeth. The final type is in-office bleaching. Not all dental offices have this equipment, but those who do apply a gel and then shine a UV light on your teeth. In about 30 minutes, you will walk out of the office with beautifully white teeth.

Cosmetic Dentistry
The most common procedure is called porcelain labial veneers. Many of us would like to change something about our smile and this is the easiest way to do so. It involves the dentist removing a very small amount (0.5mm) of tooth structure from your front teeth and replacing it with a laboratory fabricated porcelain veneer with the exact contour and shade necessary to give you that movie star smile. If you are unhappy with the appearance of your smile, definitely ask your dentist about veneers.

Terms You Should Know
We have already discussed two of the most asked about procedures, bleaching and veneers, but here are a few more:

- **Invisalign**: Chances are you have seen the ads on TV for these invisible braces. Basically, it involves wearing a series of night guards, custom made by your dentist or orthodontist. Many adults choose this option because, let's face it, it's hard to get dates with the smile of a 12-year-old pre-pubescent boy.

- **Dental Implants**: If you haven't heard of implants yet, you will. In simple terms, these are titanium screws that are placed into bone. After allowing some healing time, the implants can be restored with single crowns, bridges, or even full dentures. The advantage of implants is that they have a very high success rate (92- 99%), and with proper at-home care, they only need to be done once in your life, as opposed to traditional crowns, which have a more limited lifespan. If you are missing teeth due to decay, gum disease, trauma, or failed root canals, ask your dentist about this option.

HELPFUL WEB SITES

- www.ada.org
- www.implantingsmiles.com
- www.crest.com
- www.invisalign.com

Eye Care Tips

Have you had all the carrots that you can eat? Want to be able to read the fine print on your next ab machine purchase? Then, you really should take care of your eyes — below are some hints to help you out.

Picking An Eye Doctor

Get recommendations, look for board certifications, ask about reputations, and make sure they fit your insurance plan. You may also want to check out the American Academy of Ophthalmology and the yellow pages. Also, find out if they are on staff at quality hospitals.

Location

Make sure when choosing any doctor that their location and hours work for you. Find out if they have evening or Saturday hours, so you don't have to miss work.

During The Exam

Make sure you get a complete exam, which should include: 1) vision check to see if you need glasses, contact lenses or a change of prescription, 2) pressure check for glaucoma, 3) an examination of the front of your eye with a microscope, and 4) an examination of the back of your eyes, including the retina and nerve.

Questions And Answer

Feel free to ask as many questions as you want and make sure to tell the doctor of all medical conditions.

Cost

Usually any medical condition or injury is covered by insurance. Regular check-ups and refractions (checking the need for glasses) are not usually covered. Cost of exam will vary throughout the country. Complete exams by a board certified ophthalmologist may run $100-150. Follow ups are typically $75-100.

Lasik

LASer In-situ Keratomileusis is the reshaping of the front of the eye (cornea) to get rid of nearsightedness, farsightedness and moderate amounts of astigmatism. Lasik is a highly successful elective surgery, with about 1 million performed a year. These procedures are usually not covered by insurance. There is a risk of loss of vision, glare, dry eyes, and other results. Make sure prior to Lasik, or any other surgery, that you are fully aware of the risks and benefits of the procedure. Costs are usually $2,500-4,000 for both eyes. Don't try to save a few bucks here — go to someone you trust who will not cut corners. Remember that most people 40 and older will still need reading glasses.

Ophthalmologist vs. Optometrist

"Ophthalmologists" have a higher educational background, having completed undergrad, medical school, an internship and residency in Ophthalmology. Ophthalmologists are surgeons, medical experts of diseases of the eye, and in most cases, conduct general eye health exams and checks for glasses and contacts. "Optometrists" often refer to themselves as "Dr." — they have a Ph.D. in optometry, but they do not have a medical degree. Most optometrists deal mainly with normal, healthy eye exams. They also check and sell glasses/contact lenses.

HELPFUL WEB SITES

- www.aao.org
- www.allaboutvision.com/conditions
- www.nei.nih.gov/health/index.htm
- www.fda.gov/cdrh/lasik

Tips For Finding & Dealing With A Physician

Are you finally free of your school's health services? Finally need to graduate from the pediatrician? If so, here are some pointers to help you find a doc.

How To Pick A Physician

Important considerations are recommendations of friends, reputation, location, and availability for visits outside your work hours (i.e. evening or Saturday hours). Also, ask doctors that you know for their recommendations. Remember to see if the physician is on your insurance plan.

What Is Important To You From Your Doctor?

You want a doctor who can communicate well. Also, make sure that your doctor is up to date with technology and medicines. Does she/he publish a lot or speak for professional organizations? Think about the age and experience of your doctor. Are you more comfortable with someone older, and possibly more experienced, or would a younger, possibly more up to date doctor, who you may be able to build a longer relationship with, be a better match?

Health Insurance

- HMO's (Health Maintenance Organization) are local health management companies that usually have discounted prices for using only a limited number of doctors and specific hospitals in an area. The general advantage of an HMO is lower insurance rates, less co-payments and lower or no deductible at the doctor's office. This obviously is good for someone who is on a limited budget and/or young and in excellent health and probably doesn't see or need a doctor very often. If you are with an HMO or specific health plan you may need to call the health provider (HMO) directly for a list of providers in your area.

- PPO's (Preferred Provider Organizations) allow patients to choose from a much larger network of doctors. With PPO's your choice of doctors and hospitals is usually much larger. For a larger choice of doctors, your monthly rates are usually higher and your co-payments and deductible are usually higher. This might be a better choice for someone with complicated medical history or who feels strongly about having a lot of choices, especially when needing specialists.

How Often Should I See A Doctor?

There is no perfect answer for this question. In general, healthy young persons in their 20's and 30's should probably be seen every 2-3 years for a general exam. Those with strong family histories of diabetes, cancer, high blood pressure, high cholesterol, obesity and other diseases should be seen more often.

How To Make An Appointment

Doctors are often booked weeks to months in advance, so for a general exam call at least a month ahead. In the case of a new illness, advise the receptionist that you need to be seen soon. If you are truly miserable, say you need to be seen today and, if necessary, ask to speak to a nurse or doctor in the office. In case of an emergency, most doctors have emergency instructions on how to reach them or to go to a nearby emergency room. If it truly is an emergency and you cannot reach the doctor or your insurance company, do not worry about your insurance as your bills will likely be covered wherever you go.

HELPFUL WEB SITES

- www.webmd.com
- http://dir.yahoo.com/Health
- www.ama-assn.org/ama/pub/category/3158.html

Selecting A Lawyer

While we've all told or heard a good lawyer joke (like the one where the lawyer . . .), there won't be any laughs coming when you realize that you need to go to court or start a business. Below are some tips for finding some good legal guidance.

When Do You Need An Attorney?
While you may think that attorneys are only necessary for court appearances, you will want one to help draft a will, help review contracts, or buy a house.

Rates
Most attorneys bill on an hourly basis, usually billing a minimum of 1/10 of an hour (6 minutes). Their rates will vary depending on their area of expertise and their legal experience. Rates may start at $150/hour. You may be able to save money by having young associates and paralegals work on your matters.

How To Find An Attorney
A good way to find an attorney is through recommendations. Ask parents and friends for attorneys that they would use on their own work. You can also call your local bar association, as most have a referral office, which will put you in touch with local licensed attorneys.

Questions To Ask Prospective Attorney
You will want to discuss billing practices, such as hourly rates, how often bills are sent, and what expenses (copying, faxing, long distance) you'll be billed for. If you're dealing with special areas such as patent or tax law, you'll want to consult an attorney that specializes in such areas. Who will be working on your matter should also be discussed. Will paralegals be doing tasks at their hourly rate, which is lower, or will they have a young associate do it? You may also want to discuss what other types of law the firm handles for future legal issues.

Choosing An Attorney
It is important that you feel comfortable with your attorneys and that you trust them. Remember that they will be representing you and your reputation. Their decisions may make a significant impact on your life, whether monetarily or liberty wise in a criminal matter. You want to be able to communicate with your attorney and feel that they are there to guide you. Feel free to ask for references and check professional publications and ratings lists. Check out the offices to see if people are working hard or just hanging around. It is appropriate to get your relationship in writing, as a retainer letter is common practice.

" *The leading rule for the lawyer, as for the man of every other calling, is diligence. Leave nothing for tomorrow which can be done today...* *"*

Abraham Lincoln

HELPFUL WEB SITES

- www.abanet.org
- www.lawyers.com
- www.lawquote.com

BUYING BLING BLING, ICE, & OTHER
ROCKIN' GIFTS

gift shopping and ideas

how to buy a diamond

buying jewelry

section
08

Gift Shopping & Ideas

Got a friend getting out of the pokey? Want to give him a gift to help make up for the last 10 years in jail? That's a tough one. Better look elsewhere for help. If, however, you want to get a birthday or housewarming gift, then we've got some tips for you.

Tips

- **Money, Sales, etc.**
  How much do you want to spend on the gift? Decide how much you want to spend before going shopping, so that you don't get talked into spending more. Also, plan your gift shopping around sales so you can get more for you money (don't be afraid to stock up on other gifts if the sale is great.)

- **Wrapping**
  See if the store offers free wrapping, or if you can pay an extra buck or two to get it wrapped, saving you the hassle.

- **Special Places**
  You don't have to spend a lot to get a great present. Believe it or not, you can go to a dollar store and get a bunch of random gifts, and then give them in a cool looking receptacle, whether it be a paint can from a hardware store or a basket.

- **Save a Bunch**
  If it looks like you are going to spend a lot at a certain store, see if you are eligible for discounts by signing up for the store credit card.

Ideas

- **Food/Drinks**
  If the recipient is a food lover consider sending/bringing nice jams, bottles of wine or champagne, or finding a neat online store that sells things such as food baskets, nice baked goods, or candies.

- **Jewelry**
  What type of jewelry depends on your budget and the age/sex of the recipient.

- **Plants/Flowers**
  If you're looking for a nice, quality arrangement, think about calling a local hotel and ask for recommendations for florists.

- **Instant Lottery Tickets**
  This could be the only dollar gift you ever buy worth a million dollars.

- **Magazine Subscriptions**
  You can find a magazine to fit everyone's interests and personalities.

- **Memberships**
  Think about getting a membership to museums, planetariums, or athletic clubs.

- **Gift Cards**
  There is nothing wrong with a decent gift card or coupon. Just don't choose a place that is hard to get to or is ready to file for bankruptcy. Many online stores offer gift cards, as do some credit card companies (they work just like a debit card). You can also get mall gift certificates.

HELPFUL WEB SITES

- www.candysapples.com
- www.clearbrookfarms.com
- www.giftideacenter.com
- www.surprise.com
- www.mastercard.com
- www.tiffany.com
- www.saksfifthavenue.com
- www.chelseapaper.com
- www.simon.com/giftcard
- www.mastercard.com/us/personal/en/aboutourcards/gift_prepaid/index.html

How To Buy A Diamond

Have you always imagined that your first big purchase after getting a job would be big, red, and have 300 horses under the hood? Maybe you should rethink those horses, and consider carats instead. Here is a quick guide to help you buy a diamond.

Choose A Jeweler You Can Trust
You can't hope to understand the subtleties of diamonds without lengthy study. If possible, trust someone with whom your friends or family have done business with for a long time. You should always get recommendations from friends who have bought diamonds recently.

Finding A Jeweler
Choose a jeweler who operates out of a storefront and has a local reputation. There are more ways to be cheated than you can imagine. Established businesses are usually interested in the long run and establishing a relationship with you.

Don't Kid Yourself
Be honest with yourself and the jeweler about your budget for your purchase.

Getting A Deal
Understand that there is not a big mark-up on diamonds. So, when a jeweler offers you a fabulous price, run the other way. There are no bargains in diamonds - just diamonds that for some hidden reason command less money.

Carrot Or Carat?
Understand that a carat isn't a size, it's a weight. Just as a 100-pound girl can be 5' tall or 5'5, so can diamonds vary greatly in their dimensions per weight.

Diamond Color
Remember that diamond color is graded upside down, through the culet (the pointy part at the bottom). Most diamonds can face up (the way we use them) up to two grades better or worse than the upside down grade. But the grade of record is the upside down grade. If it's a great price, could be it faces up lower than the upside down grade.

Clarity
Similarly, clarity is not graded by eye, nor is it graded by microscope. It's graded with a 10 power loupe or the equivalent. You should not hypothetically be able to see the difference between a VS and an SI clarity with the naked eye. If you can see the inclusion with the naked eye, it's an I grade.

Appraisal

A reputable jeweler should provide a detailed appraisal with your ring. After you receive the ring and appraisal, you need to purchase insurance, which, in the case of a loss, will replace or repair your ring exactly as it was. Agreed amount insurance is a little more expensive, but worth it.

Luxury, Not Investment

Jewelry does not necessarily appreciate over time. It is not an investment, it's a luxury and a pleasure. Diamonds are a commodity, and their prices are subject to market variations, as well as the fluctuation in new finds.

Payment

Buying a diamond is like buying a car - no one pays the list price, they are all negotiable. So shop around and see who will offer you the best deal. You can almost always put the ring on a payment plan so you won't have to come up with a large chunk of cash up-front. Plus, there are 0% interest credit cards out there that will allow you to purchase now and pay later with a whole year without interest.

HELPFUL WEB SITES

- www.borislitwin.com
- www.adiamondisforever.com
- www.debeers.com
- www.mondera.com/diamonds

Buying Jewelry

How do you find the perfect bling bling for that special friend? There are a few questions to keep in mind. Consider his/her age, style, and your budget.

Age
Be sure to keep the gift recipient's age in mind. You don't want to be seeing your 80-year-old grandmother wearing a "Best Friends Forever" heart necklace.

Budget
You can find lots of great jewelry at a low price. There are always sales going on at your local department stores. Don't be afraid to check out the flea markets. You can even make it yourself! Get yourself some wire or thread and go to a bead store or craft store. If you don't have much time on your hands to bead strands and strands of necklaces, think about just purchasing one cool large bead or rock. Hey, you might even have some wicked shells that you collected on a beach vacation that you could slip onto some wire.

Vacation
It can be fun to combine your vacation memories with gifts. If you're at a beach town or visiting an exotic place that has some local flavor in their jewelry, take a risk and purchase some. It is always fun to think that your friends remembered you even when they were off in a far off place.

Style
This is a fine line to walk. You want to give the gift recipient a present that they'll want to wear and not just open the gift wearing that plastered on smile and forced thank you. To avoid this, be sure to keep his/her taste in mind. Try to find a nice balance between your personal style and theirs. It is always fun to receive a present that you would not necessarily buy for yourself because you might be scared to try a new look. If you and your friend have totally different styles, try to buy the piece of jewelry keeping 75 % of the recipient's personal style in mind and 25% yours. Even if they're more into the frumpy look and you're not, they'll be more likely to wear something that is up their alley and no matter what, they'll think about you when they wear it.

Occasion
Do you want your friend to wear this piece of jewelry everyday or just on a special occasion? This topic often goes hand in hand with budget.

> *" Regard your good name as the richest jewel you can possibly be possessed of... "*

Socrates

HELPFUL WEB SITES

- www.ftc.gov/bcp/conline/pubs/products/jewelry.htm
- http://jewelry.about.com
- www.bbb.org/alerts/article.asp?ID=441

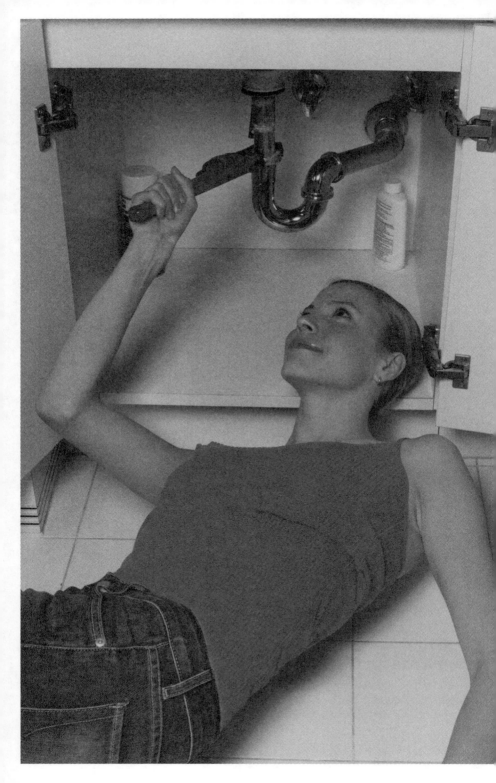

KITCHEN SINK

important dates

general stuff

financial stuff

notes

section
09

Important Dates

Put your important dates below so you'll never forget.

Jan
_____ _____
_____ _____
_____ _____
_____ _____

Feb
_____ _____
_____ _____
_____ _____
_____ _____

Mar
_____ _____
_____ _____
_____ _____
_____ _____

Apr
_____ _____
_____ _____
_____ _____
_____ _____

May
_____ _____
_____ _____
_____ _____
_____ _____

Jun
_____ _____
_____ _____
_____ _____
_____ _____

Jul

Aug

Sep

Oct

Nov

Dec

General Stuff

	Name/Carrier	Phone #'s
Doctor		( )
Dentist		( )
Car Insurance		( )
Renter's Insurance		( )
Health Insurance		( )
Cable		( )
Gas		( )
Electricity		( )
Cell Phone		( )

Financial Stuff

NOTE: Be careful with your account numbers - make up a code for your numbers, ex: add 1 to every number.

	PIN #'s	Phone #'s
Stock Brocker		( )
Credit Card 1		( )
Credit Card 2		( )
Credit Card 3		( )
Credit Card 4		( )
Credit Card 5		( )
Credit Card 6		( )
Checking Account		( )
Savings Account		( )

Notes

Notes

Notes

Notes

Graduate Survival Guide

Notes

Notes

Graduate Survival Guide

Notes

Notes

Graduate Survival Guide

Notes

This book would not have been possible without the brilliant and insightful help from the following people:

David Dorfman	Arielle Sandler	Ben Pugh
Matt Ziegler	Jamie Kull	Lee Robinson
Jeremy Berry	Emmy Wohlgemuth	Carolyn Bregman
Jonathan Buka	Dan Klepal	Jennifer Ross
James Young	Sasha Carp	Scott Silver
Ian Collazo	Naomi Greenfield	William Spinnenweber
Stephen Wu	Annsley Hillman	Ryan Streight
Jason Edgecombe	Max Leinwand	Eric Toth
Kira Frank	Steven Licardi	Melissa Klein
Alexis Bergman	Jeff Nelson	Kathy Bergman
BJ Foreman	Jordan Pelchovitz	Hillary Stewart
Susan Gainen	Eric Leib	Howard Richshafer
Earl Crane	Anna Proctor	Estee Liebross
Stephen Hartz	Thomas Bergman	Spencer Preis
Clay Holloway	Deborah Levi	Jill McGrail
Richard Klein	Susie Bradford	

Thank you.

The Man Behind The Book

Michael Bergman, Creator

Michael received his B.S.B.A. from the John M. Olin School of Business at Washington University in St. Louis and his J.D. from Emory University School of Law. Besides creating the Graduate Survival Guide, Michael created and licensed Numbskull - The SAT Prep Game and successfully operated Bare Ware, LLC. He is currently working on several new projects.

If you have any comments regarding the book or any ideas for new topics feel free to email us at info@gradsurvival.com and remember to visit us on the web.

www.gradsurvival.com